RUGBY STORIES

RUGBY STORIES

Some rucking good yarns

Peter FitzSimons

ALLEN & UNWIN

First published in 1993
Allen & Unwin Pty Ltd
9 Atchison Street, St Leonards, NSW 2065 Australia

National Library of Australia
Cataloguing-in-Publication entry:

FitzSimons, Peter.
  Rugby stories.

  ISBN 1 86373 440 6

  1. FitzSimons, Peter—Anecdotes. 2. FitzSimons, Peter—Humor.
  3. Rugby Union football—Anecdotes. I. Title.

796.333

Set in 11/12.5 Palatino by DOCUPRO, Sydney
Printed by Australian Print Group, Maryborough, Victoria

10 9 8 7 6 5 4 3 2

To my late father, Peter McCloy FitzSimons.
A good man with a great love of rugby.

CONTENTS

10 OUR LEAGUE COUSINS

INTRODUCTION

One time, I was driving along behind this car heading out of my French village, and this dog just like Fred Bassett had its head out the window. As the car sped up the dog's ears began to flap back and forth into its eyes, slowly at first and then faster and harder, and then its tongue too began to beat harder and harder back and forth, and still the dog didn't pull its head in even when we hit the freeway and were really motoring.

I suspect the dog no more knew why he was doing such a seemingly silly thing than most of us know why we play rugby. The pounding he was taking be damned, he was just having the most HELLUVA time a dawg ever had, and if he had been suddenly turned into a human I'm confident that he would soon have gravitated to the rugby field.

My own gravitation to the game started young. Back on the farm when I was growing up, my three brothers went away one after the other to boarding school in Sydney and returned home with news of the game. When I got older, Dad would take me down to see them play and tell me stories of his own experiences in the game, playing at that same school in the 1930s and then with the Army during the Second World War.

One thing led to another, led to my own departure for school and learning the game, led to playing at Sydney University, led to spending five years in Italy and France as a rugby nomad, led to playing with the Wallabies, led to the collection of stories gathered in this book.

I don't love the game itself as much as you might expect of someone with such a background, though there is something about it I at least like a lot. Mostly I guess, I love what has gone with it—colour and movement, travel, glory, lasting friendships, rich memories and that certain sense of *timelessness* that goes with the game.

I hope that some measure of that lot is contained in this book.

Peter Fitz.
Annandale.
Wee hours.
February '93

1 A COUPLE OF FAVOURITES

KISS-AND-MIST RUGBY IS THE LATIN FASHION

Her name was Kathy and my name was Peter and we were in an extremely competitive relationship. On Monday, 25 May, 1986, she told me she was going to be published in the **Herald** *that Thursday in their 'Relations' column, a readers' contribution section of the paper.*

How could I beat her and get published sooner? It so happened that the Italian rugby side was then in town about to play a Test match against the Wallabies and a year earlier I had played a seasons rugby in Italy. Perhaps if I wrote a story on Italian rugby they would print it?

The Sports Editor of the **Herald** *at the time, Tom Hammond, was non-committal but said he'd look it over if I wrote it, which was enough for me. I took two days break from my job, labouring for a landscaper friend of mine between European rugby seasons, and wrote it literally night and day, submitting it on the Wednesday evening.*

On Thursday it tragically did not appear, but then again Kathy's 'Relations' column had been held over till the following week, so it was okay. On Friday it was my job to go to the local shop and get morning tea for the other labourers, and with the same tremulous hand of the day before, I opened the **Sydney Morning Herald** *to the sports section.*

Top of the back page was the article that follows, word for word as I had written it. My fellow labourers had to wait for their play-lunch while I worked the phones—'have you seen the **Herald** *today? Quickly, go and get a copy!'*

Plunging through mist late in the second half on a frozen field in Rovigo, Italy, it suddenly hit me that there really isn't much in common between the game played in Italy and the one played in Australia.

Perhaps of all the sports played internationally rugby is the one that bears most distinctively in substance and style of play the national characteristics of each country. Played worldwide with exactly the same rules and regulations, it is a hybrid plant that grows differently in each country according to the ground in which it is nurtured.

With the arrival of the Italian rugby team in this country and the forthcoming Test match at Ballymore, the Australian rugby public will get a rare chance to see rugby as it has grown in Italy.

Having played one very enjoyable season in Italian rugby I believe I can give some description of the way in which their game and style of play has arisen.

Despite the relative lack of recognition internationally the Italian game is flourishing in its natural habitat and has a loyal following from town to town, particularly in the north. The most distinctive feature of the game there is the emotionally charged atmosphere in which each match is played.

Whereas in the Sydney championship there are ten first division teams training and playing in the same city, in Italy each of the major towns has its own team and the championship is truly national from Sicily to Venice (where you can play only at low tide).

When I was there it was not unlike seeing modern-day warriors doing battle each Sunday afternoon for the honour of the town. In the Churchillian speeches that preceded every match we were continually exhorted to new heights against the heathen mob that awaited us and a loss, particularly on home turf, was catastrophic.

Our team, like most in the championship, was three times the side when we were playing at home in front of friends and family. I first became aware of the depth of this emotion fairly early in the season when we scored a narrow win over an invading team regarded as a traditional rival. At the final whistle, instead of the round of handshakes and 'thanks for the game' I was used to, I was suddenly awash in hugs, tears and kisses among my team-mates.

Being true blue, I was shocked. But on considering the 'when in Rome' adage I changed my mind and quickly got right into it. A similar theme was being played out between the 4000–5000 spectators in the stands and I remember reflecting at the time that it was a long, long way from sunny Manly Oval on a Saturday afternoon.

The weather also seemed a little bizarre to this Australian boy. Playing and practising on the snow in below-zero temperatures became normal and there evolved, of course, a series of tactics and strategies to be used when it was snowing. More interesting, though, was the game when it was played in heavy mist.

My host town, Rovigo (just south of Venice), was genuinely the mist capital of southern Europe, being situated between two rivers and the Adriatic.

On several occasions the mist was so heavy that opposing five-eighths could not even see each other. But no matches were ever stopped because of the mist and visibility—or the lack thereof—became part of the strategy.

In that situation of thick swirling mist the strategy was for we forwards to secure the ball the best we could and give it to our five-eighth, Stefano Betarello, who is also the Italian five-eighth. He, not unlike John Bertrand coming down the final stretch of the America's Cup course looking for a hopeful patch of wind, would direct play towards the thickest part of the mist.

When the opposition had the ball those of us cover-defending would have to head out into the wilderness on a search-and-destroy mission for the ball carrier and just keep in touch with each other the best we could. And the spectators? What spectators, officer?

Needless to say, none of the experience gained by the Italians playing in these kinds of conditions will be of use to them at Ballymore, Nevertheless, I do believe the Italians have the potential to do a lot better than they have been given credit for in the lead-up games to this Test. Realistically, the Italians cannot hope to win, but if the ball bounces their way it could be an interesting spectacle.

Their forwards may be characterised, to borrow from Banjo Paterson, as having 'mightly little science but a mightly lot of dash', while the backs have their fair share of whatever that mysterious wellspring is that makes Latin sporting teams so unpredictable, creative and sometimes brilliant.

Although much has been made of the relative difference in size between the formidable Australian pack and the diminutive Italians, there will also be a problem, I think, because of shortcomings in technique. For example, in contrast to the seemingly endless discussions we have here about scrums concerning feet positions, synchronisation, wrist tightening etc, there we were lucky if we ever saw the scrum machine let alone talk about technique. The result was that scrums were usually as chaotically unorganised as a dropped plate of spaghetti and I would expect the weakest point of the Italian forwards' game in fact to be the scrum.

In the line-outs the Italians should again be dominated, but for the rest, their dash should hold them in good stead and they should get at least some supply of ball for the backs. As to the latter, on their day they can be breathtakingly innovative and creative.

I suppose the most likely scenario is that this creativeness, and sometimes brilliance, will be firmly crushed by the troops sent up by General Jones, but if the Italian backs fire early it could be difficult for the Australians to keep up to the point-a-minute task set by the good general.

AND NOW, REAL RUGBY GREATS

Every year it's the same thing. At the end of the season the world's rugby journalists always release their own WORLD XVs—the best rugby team that could be formed if you could pick all the players you could find in every mud heap all over the planet. It is, not to put too fine a point on it, a boring journalistic cliché that should long ago have been put beneath the sod. Particularly when no one has ever seen fit to put *you* in one . . .

What we *really* need is a World XV made up not just from the players of the moment, but more interestingly, from the great players of history—since the beginning of time. So let's go . . .

Physio: Jesus Christ
No football team can be without a good physiotherapist. And in all history one physio stands above all others . . .

Forget the old saying 'it hasn't happened since JC played full-back for Jerusalem'. Yes, yes, yes, of course JC *was* a helluva full-back and Jerusalem *did* win the Holy Grail when he was their No. 15. We all know that. But I want you to forget JC's sidestep. I want you to forget his amazing ability to open up opposition defences like they were the Red Sea (just as that famous old five-eighth Moses taught him). The *real* talent of JC lay in his ability as a physiotherapist.

His fantastic healing powers are still legend at the Jerusalem Rugby Club. You say the prop has done his cruciate and medial ligaments all in one go and will most probably never play again? Can't even *walk* you say? JC! Get over here! See what you can do for the prop, would you?

And wouldn't you know it? JC would lay his hands upon him, and without so much as wincing with pain the prop is up and *running*! Ready to charge through walls and tear into them in the second half. The most incredible thing you've ever seen, I tell you.

(Incidentally, the other thing about having JC with the team is that he does a terrific little number as after-match caterer. I swear that one time there were 50 000 people at a Jerusalem–Bethlehem Grand Final and somehow, with only a couple of loaves and fish, sprinkled liberally with the remains of Lot's wife, JC fed the whole damn lot of them.)

Loose-head prop and captain: Winston Churchill

His strength in adversity is absolutely proven and he has more or less the right physique. But those qualities are just a bonus.

Imagine this: Mars (or whoever we're going to put this team up against) scores a high intercept try under the posts to make the World XV twenty points behind with only fifteen minutes to go.

The chips are down. Who else are you going to get to make the speech to the troops under the goalposts at a time like this? Who else but Winston, of course. If he were to give *you* the ol' 'We shall defend our island . . . the World XV shall *never* surrender' bit under the goalposts with fifteen minutes to go, wouldn't *you* want to go out and give the Martians a fearful drubbing?

And make no mistake, he'd also give a *great* after-match speech.

Hooker: Benito Mussolini

What a player. What a guy. Like any good hooker he has a streak of viciousness in him as wide as a runway. He's bull-headed. He's squat. He's ugly. He's pretty good at cheating without being obvious about it. All prime requisites. There's the obvious problem with Benny that he'd always be trying to seize power from Winston in a big coup, but Winnie would be equal to it. Benny's our boy.

Tight-head prop: Buddha

The anchor of the scrum. The cornerstone. As every follower knows, what every team needs in its pack of forwards is a guy who, though he may not be very mobile, is

8

big and strong and beefy and just won't move come what may. Trust me, Buddha is the man for the job. He has the physique. He has the moral strength and the character. Many of you might think he's a bit quiet, a bit of a pacifist, that he's not aggressive enough, but you gotta understand—we can't have a whole team of Churchills. Every team *needs* a strong silent type who doesn't say much, but who can keep the team on a steady keel whether it's 40 points up or *down*. Buddha is such a man.

Left second-rower: Charles de Gaulle

I know it's a big call, but I have to go with Charlie on this one. He's big, he's strong, he's a *winner*. He just doesn't know when he's beat and beat badly. Sure, like Benny he's got a tendency to disregard totally who the captain is, and I know he positively *insists* on making endless speeches, but the point is Charlie *finds a way to win*.

Why, I remember the time he was playing for France against the Germans. The Jerries had it all over the Froggies and were winning by hundreds of points. They just kept shellacking the French from deep inside the Froggies' own territory. Did he quit? Did he *hell*. He left the field briefly, got hold of a loudspeaker and started inciting the crowd to riot. Pretty soon there was carnage everywhere, but the French got up in a close one.

Right second-rower: Goliath

Has to be. Stick him in the middle of the line-out, jumping at No. 4 and Golly Goliath will be a sure-fire winner. I know Golly has had at least one notable defeat in the past—in another sport—but I swear that little wimp David got him with what can only be described as a *cheap shot*.

You shouldn't go thinking Golly's no sportsman just because of that. Also, Golly pushing behind Buddha in the scrum would be unbeatable—the perfect combination of physical and moral strength.

Right breakaway: Genghis Khan

Exactly what the World XV of history needs—a little tearaway warrior who just won't quit. The thing you need in a breakaway is a guy who *likes* a fight, a scrap, a biff.

A guy who doesn't feel quite himself if, after five minutes into the game, he doesn't have a little bit of blood just dribbling down his nose on to his lip, and his eyebrow isn't swelling up. I tell you Genghis is our man. I've seen him play and across the tundra there's no one like him. With the wind in his hair, the glint in his eye, the fierce imprecations springing from his lips, nobody can put the wind up the opposing full-back under the high-ball like Genghis Khan can. Usually, just the *sight* of Genghis closing in is enough to make the bloke drop the ball.

Left breakaway: Che Guevara

On this one, I want to talk less about Che, who I think picks himself, and more about why I didn't go for the other obvious contender for the spot.

A lot of people out there think that I should pick Adolf Hitler for left breakaway, because of his speed, his aggression and the way he's so brilliant in destroying the opposition defence by doing his blitzkrieg thing where the five-eighth puts the ball up behind the lines and before you know it that crazy little German is there creating absolute havoc.

Fair enough, but there's still a serious problem. Adolf gives away too many penalties. We all know it; Adolf has no respect for the rules of the game. There is even some question as to whether he even *knows* the rules in the first place. If we wanted somebody to gouge the opposition in the eyeballs, to kick them in the head when they are down, and to give them big king hits from behind, then Adolf is our man. But we don't. Guys like that cost too many points, create too much bad feeling, and are just too much hassle.

Adolf is not in the team. Not now, not ever, and I don't want to hear any more about it.

So Che gets the job.

No. 8: Saddam Hussein

Saddam is a bit wild and can be a bit embarrassing at after-match functions. He's also a fraction short and squat, and we might be giving something away in the line-out by choosing him. But *never a better No. 8 pulled on a boot*. He's just the guy we need. Not only does he have that streak of craziness in him that you often see in the very very best of footballers, but the guy is above all a survivor who just refuses to be intimidated come what may.

I don't care if it turns out that the Mars XV are ten metres tall with arms as thick as thighs, and thighs as big as oak trees. If it comes to a stoush, Saddie the Baddie won't back off one inch I tell ya, even if the whole lot of them get Saddam into the mother of all corners and pound the living daylights out of him for maybe as long as half the game. Somehow, unbelievably, Saddie will survive and live to belt another day.

Half-back: Aristotle
A thinker. A communicator. The half-back must be both these things. He must be able to work out in a split second what the right option is and then set his backline in motion to achieve his purpose. And he must communicate to all around him just what is going on.

It's gotta be Ari. Not only was he a great thinker, he practically *invented* thinking in the first place. Why, if he hadn't been around maybe they wouldn't even have thought of football. And then where would we be? We'd be *stuffed* is where we'd be. But the bottom line is, we *owe* it to Ari to give him a run.

Five-eighth: John F. Kennedy
There is something of an unwritten law in Rugby Union that the five-eighth has got to be a basically good-looking sort of bloke. A bit like the quarter-back in gridiron. Guys with broken noses, gnarled features and scarred faces need not apply. Instead, you need a suave sort of guy who can play 80 minutes in the mud and still look like a million dollars.

You see, when you line up before the kick-off there are two things guys look at in the opposing team: have they got big gnarled second-rowers and have they got a good-looking five-eighth?

Well, we've got the big gnarled second-rowers, but where are we going to get a better looking five-eighth than JFK? The answer is, we're not. So he's got the job.

11

Inside centre: Napoleon Bonaparte

Of course he's the obvious choice for the mid-field general. The way Boney reads the game is nothing short of sensational. In two seconds flat he can see the opposition's weak point and then frame an attack that will exploit it.

I know he made a few mistakes at the big match at Waterloo last century and his confidence was down a bit after that one, but I've talked to him and I think he can be persuaded to get his boots back on one more time.

Also, forget the fact that Charlie de Gaulle keeps nattering on that Boney is an 'over-rated little pip-squeak' and shouldn't be in the team. I think we will have to overrule Charlie on this one. Boney is not only in, he's also vice-captain.

Outside centre: Attila the Hun

Now as everybody who knows anything about rugby knows, if we're going to have a guy like Boney playing at inside centre—a guy who basically is so full of guile and wiles and sidesteps and trickery that it's not *true*; someone who is so skilled that he sometimes maybe even forgets to go forward—then we're going to need a hard nut to make the hard yards outside him. Attila the Hun is my choice for centre. If Boney can't put Attie through a few gaps, then I promise you Attila will finish the job and he can also be counted on to make a few big hits in defence as well. Attila's the man. ATTA BOY!

Right-winger: Margaret Thatcher

Who else are we going to put to the right of Attila the Hun? Maggie practically invented modern right-wing play on her own so no one can hold a candle to her. Some might say that as a woman she might not be strong enough to cope, but they are the sexist, chauvinistic morons, who bleated like that for years while she was in office, and she'll do to the opposition what she did to them: streamroller them regardless.

Left-winger: Vladimir Lenin

Way, way out there on the left wing, right to the very extremes, you never saw a better left-winger than Vladimir.

He really 'cuts 'em up'. I know what you're thinking. You're thinking he's been looking a bit green around the gills lately, that he hasn't been looking at all well. That lying in state in Moscow for the past 67 years doesn't agree with his constitution, but I think if we get JC on the job we should be able to get him right for the big day.

JC has done it before and I'm sure he'll do it again. I mean, how do you think we're going to get these other guys up and running? You think it's going to be easy getting Attila the Hun and Aristotle going again after all these years, let alone getting boots back on their now powdery feet? Jesus can handle it. As to Vladimir, there never was a better left-winger.

Full-back: Serge Blanco
Just can't go past Serge. Not only has he played more than 80 times for the fair dinkum French Test XV, and scored a zillion tries for them, but I also think he holds his place in the team across the ages. Serge for mine.

WHAT ENGLAND EXPECTS

Movies and sit-coms have special guest appearances so why can't a book? The following is, for me, one of the funniest rugby pieces ever written. It appeared at the time of the 1991 World Cup and its author, Simon Carr, has very graciously agreed to it appearing in this book.

Simon Carr calls for emergency laws to make the Aussies pay for being too flash and too Italian.

Pursuant to the second semi-final of the Rugby World Cup, and given the resultant circumstances of the Australian representatives playing England in the final of the said competition, the Board of the Rugby Football Union announces the following rule changes to be made in the laws of the game of rugby football.

Scoring

In response to public demand, the practice of running with the ball has increased without hindrance in the past ten years. This reaction to market forces is a form of professionalism and is contrary to the spirit of the establishment of rugby football. Rather than expel or suspend persistent offenders under existing laws governing amateur status, the scoring system for World Cup finals shall be amended as follows.

(a) Tries scored by fancy wingers with Italian names shall be worth 1 point.
(b) Tries scored by hard-working forwards inching an invisible ball onwards under a maul of men through a period of a quarter of an hour shall be worth 6 points.

(c) Grovelling in scrums, releasing the ball reluctantly, and immediately kicking for touch shall be worth 2 points.

Penalties

The laws concerning foul play shall be extended to cover incidents that are to be considered as dishonest in intent or against the spirit of the game. Free kicks by way of penalties shall be awarded if any player:

(a) runs forward with the ball as if to engage the opposition three-quarter line, but at the last minute chips the ball over their heads and bursts through the legitimately constructed defensive line to score under the posts. The kick shall be awarded on the grounds of wilful deception.

(b) comes in from the wing to take the ball and runs diagonally across the pitch to score. The kick shall be awarded on grounds of careless individualism.

(c) takes a kick ahead on the first bounce, wrong-foots a full-back, takes three opposition players out and throws the ball over his shoulder without looking to see if he is supported but knowing that he is, because he is an Australian of Italian descent. The kick shall be awarded for vainglory.

(d) chases a ball the length of the pitch to frighten the opposition full-back on his tryline, and 15 seconds later makes a try-saving tackle on his own line in the opposite corner. The kick shall be awarded for trying too hard.

Note: the attention of referees is specially drawn to the necessity of rigidly and immediately enforcing the new law, with particular attention to the case of fancy wingers with Italian names who run faster than a racing ostrich with a bee in its bum.

Eligibility to play

National representatives shall be expected to belong morally as well as legally to their represented country. Players with double-barrelled names shall be recognised as clearly being English. Players with names ending in -agh shall be deemed Irish and shall not be allowed to play except for Ireland. Names ending in -ese shall be deemed Italian. All nationalities shall be required to play for their morally national teams, or for England, whichever is the closer at the time of walking on to the pitch at Twickenham.

Compensatory tries

(a) After 15 minutes of almost motionless scrummaging under the posts a try in compensation shall be awarded to the attacking team.
(b) If the host team attempts three times to penetrate the opponent's defence, starting from play originating inside the 22, the third attack shall be deemed successful and be awarded a try in compensation.
(c) If the visitors score a try in the corner with three men over, there shall be a try awarded against them on grounds of excess in times of recession.

Ratification of final winners

The result of the final shall be provisional until both highest-circulating British tabloids have carried front-page admissions that Australia is culturally, economically, and sexually superior to England, and that Australia should be compensated with large cash sums for Gallipoli, nuclear testing on Australian soil, and Britain's entry into the EC.

ONE DAY IN THE LIFE OF THE DOORS OF PERCEPTION

There's this great American writer called Hunter S. Thompson, see, and what he does is get himself tanked up on whisky and all kinds of stuff and wait till 3 am when he comes in off the porch where he has been sitting nude while shooting his six-gun into the wilderness and then he just writes down what comes into his head and then he breaks all the normal rules of grammar and syntax and writing, but somehow what he comes up with is invariably very readable and sometimes brilliant or at the very least it's different.

And if the rest of us can't write like him, at least we can mimic his actions and see what comes out. So, half a bottle of whisky behind me, and 40 shots fired into the low hills of Annandale, but it's too cold to be nude so forget it, let us turn our drunken attention to sport and see what happens . . .

So what the hell is it with those soccer people? Why don't they widen the goals or something, but how come it is so all-fired difficult for them to score and so deadly boring to watch when maybe if they widened the goals it would make it more difficult for the goalie to defend and there would be more goals scored and the whole thing would be far more interesting and what do you think?

I mean the goals are pretty much as wide now as when they invented and formalised the damn game, but the goalies you see are far more able and athletic and they can leap at least twice as far as Rod Marsh used to do so what is the point of even shooting at the goal because the boogers are just too damned good . . .

And tennis. One more tennis game and I'll puke. It used to be interesting didn't it? But now it bores me rigid. There's a guy called Jakob Hlasek, I think, and he is ninth in the world or something, and he comes from Switzerland and he's ninth in the world and nobody knows or cares anything about him and how can tennis be in a healthy state if a guy called Jacob Hlasek from Switzerland is currently one of the nine best players on the *planet* and nobody knows the first damn thing about him. I ask you?

And does anybody care anymore about the Sydney Swans and why do those boogers even bother trotting out, and while we're on the subject, not that we really are, what happened to all those wonderful things they used to say about basketball? Has that game gone off the boil something serious or what?

When the basketball troops used to extrapolate their crowd figures to mid-1991, they reckoned that there'd be a pensioner couple in lower Woop-Woop with a crook car and a sick dog who might stay home one Saturday night, but just about all the rest of Australia would be at the basketball. And it hasn't happened.

And the Wallabies . . . sorry, that should read the XXXX Wallabies. Why would we stop there I ask you? Why can't we call the captain Nick Farr-XXXX-Jones and the lock Sam Scott-XXXX-Young? I mean, gee, there's nothing wrong with a bit of sponsorship here and there but you don't think we might be carrying it a tad far calling them the XXXX Wallabies do you?

As for the Australian swimming team known as the Uncle Toby's Dolphins, where the hell is this all going to stop? Next thing they'll be calling the main Rugby League trophy the Winfield Cup or something equally outrageous. And how come everything that's coming out of my pen is so damned negative? Didn't they put any positive stuff in this whisky bottle? Isn't there anything *nice* to say about sport? Yes, maybe, maybe, coming now . . . almost there . . . what about netball and, hell, maybe that's not such a bad game after all and hell I hope I get a lot of brownie points for saying that and (Waiter! More whisky!) back to being negative . . .

How come we like watching Rugby League on the box so much when basically we're seeing the same action-guy take the ball up, get belted, fall over, guy takes the ball up, get's belted, falls over—about *ten thousand* times in 80 minutes? Can't they vary it a bit?

And I seriously doubt if there's anybody out there

18

un-offended by all this, but what the hell? After that debate I did with the South African ambassador on 'A Current Affair' the other night, you can't fit any more hate mail into my pigeon-hole with a *shoe horn*, let alone anything else, so you're just wasting your time, wasting your time, wasting your time.

I hate hate mail but that's the bizzo, I suppose. I suppose. I suppose. I suppose. I don't suppose this formula for an article is wearing a bit thin is it? Well, let's stop it there. Stop it there. Stop it there, there, there, it can only get better. Waiter! More whisky!

2 PLAYING THE DIFFERENT COUNTRIES

LIFE WITH AN ALL BLACK ON YOUR BACK

It is like this . . . There you are, just minding your own business during the Test match, trying to keep out of everyone's way, when, just for the pure hell of it, you decide to dive on a loose ball. Next thing you know a maul has formed over you and you have to watch helplessly as a couple of men dressed in black use their steel-studded leather boots to write their initials all over your lily-white legs.

That is what playing the All Blacks in a Test match is like. Hard. Occasionally brutal. Damaging. And not just on your legs. There is also your back to worry about. In All Black games it is also fairly standard procedure for your own scrum to collapse while theirs does not and then you will swear, I mean you will positively swear that a giant black centipede has just danced a jig on your back.

Of all the varied sensations and impressions that one experiences on the inside of an All Black forward conglomeration, the most memorable are the All Black feet. Few players finish a game against them without a few lasting impressions on their backs and legs, and my games against them have been no exception.

In an upright position and pushing against the New Zealanders in the rucks and mauls, one sees their feet whirring around, spitting mud out behind them. Fall into that maelstrom and it feels like you are caught tying your shoelaces when the bulls of Pamplona pass through.

Sure, it is legal, most of it, but one is no less a sore little vegemite at the end of it for all that. So much for the sight and feel of the inside of the All Black pack. Smell? I guess the All Blacks smell fairly normal in a rugby sort of way. Eau de mud, sweat and vaseline . . . That sort of thing. Though at the time of my last game against them, my nose got so badly broken that I could not even thmell my own thocks let alone the inthide of the maul. I do seem to remember the usual pungent odour emanating from them just before it smashed. The sort of thing you might sprinkle on yourself if you were going on a date with a gorilla.

Sound? Groans and grunts of effort, exchanges of imprecations as the two front rows hit in the scrum, the sound of flesh hitting flesh at speed, the 'ooooph' as a player fringing the ruck gets hit by an opposing player launched from ten metres out. If there is one difference to the usual sound score it is that there always seems to be a lot of chatter coming from the All Black side of the maul.

The All Black forwards might often be described as 'a machine', but there is always a lot of communication going on between them. Not only the fairly standard 'Drive it!' and 'Take it up!' but often the more specific calls of 'Here's the ball!', 'Rip his hands off it!', 'Roll it left!' and 'Get him!'. My own favourite All Black communique came from a particularly burly forward (even by All Black standards) towards the end of the aforementioned 'steel-studded boots' game. I had rather mildly been trying to scratch my own initials into the leg of one of the All Blacks who had previously done it to me when their loosehead prop, Kevin Boroevich, caught sight of me.

Looking my way with wonder, he demanded for all the world as if he really wanted to know: 'What the hell do you think you are doing?' He looked so genuinely appalled it was all I could do to stop myself from apologising. In retrospect I am glad I did not bother. In the next ruck I received some unsolicited souvenir autographs from the entire All Black pack that I was able to admire for weeks. Even now, when the morning sun is just right, I am still able to admire the remnants of a few of my more treasured autographs right there in the small of my back.

Of course, the Wallaby–All Black matches are tough games. Always have been. Traditionally, two of the toughest brands of football you can play are Test matches and local derbies. When you combine the two as in the trans-Tasman encounters between us and them, the ferocity of the clashes is inevitably the stuff of legend. Sunday's semifinal match, of course, will be the first time the teams have met beyond the bounds of Australasia, but the ferocity will no doubt be undiminished for all that. And yet, and yet, there are a lot of ties between our two nations . . .

Most particularly because, if the truth be known, with New Zealand's current dire economic straits, most Kiwis actually live over in Sydney—no kidding. The fifteen All Blacks might just be the last people left living in the Land of the Long White Cloud. These days the standing instructions of parting New Zealanders to those left behind is: 'Don't forget, last one out, turn the lights off.' It is rather a moot point whether, with the All Blacks presently in Ireland, the lights are on or off. Did Gary Whetton remember to flick the switch when he left Auckland airport?

And yet, there were at least a few New Zealanders when the Wallabies toured last year. I know that, because in a moment of rare generosity, the Australian selectors picked me as a member of the touring party. I suppose it was then, immediately we landed at Auckland, that we Australians really gathered what a strange, strange bunch the New Zealanders are. From the baggage claim through the customs hall and out to the airport lounge, every Kiwi we passed murmured to us to 'Watch out for the blicks', 'The blicks are waiting for you, you know', and 'Wait till the blicks are finished with you lot', etc. etc.

What were they on about? With consternation in our hearts we formed our luggage trolleys up into a wagon train and headed for the bus, all the while looking out for the mysterious blicks. We did not know who or what they were, but we did not like the sound of them.

Finally, in the safety of the bus, with our big prop Ewan McKenzie jammed up hard against the door, we demanded some answers from the Kiwi bus driver. Who exactly were these blicks and what did they have against us? With a look of complete astonishment, the bus driver fairly burst out with 'Are you *kidding*? The blicks, the blicks, the AWL BLICKS!'

Well, we thought it was funny, anyway.

25

PLAYING RUGBY'S GENTLEMEN

In June of 1989, I think it was, I had the pleasure of playing for the Australia B team against the Lions. It was quite something to cross swords with the best of British, as I recall . . .

'Aahhrrr, it's yoooo argenn, yer big *oaf*!!!' John Jeffrey, the Scottish breakaway, screamed at me as we clashed once more in the middle of a muddy maul. 'Coom orn then laddie, let's goo fer it!'

Which meant, I surmised, that he thought a bit of biffo might be the order of the day. I did too, but was rather nonplussed at his extension of a formal invitation. This is a far from usual procedure in international rugby matches. The All Blacks signal for the fight to begin is usually a crashing blow from a big right hand. The French and Italians tend to send their fight invitations wrapped in a swinging boot. We Australians like to yell things such as 'Oh yeah!?! Well cop this then!' before setting to.

But this was the British Lions. While calling them gentlemen would be an exaggeration, they seemed to be not a bad equivalent in rugby terms. Attempts at under-handed physical intimidation were not—in this match at least—part of their repertoire. While they tackled hard and rucked ferociously, no other dastardly derring-do emerged. A fight could occur if the occasion warranted, but playing simple hard rugby seemed to be their main preoccupation.

Typically, just as Jeffrey and I were squaring off for the first round of our own bout, he happened to glimpse the ball in British hands up-field, and without a word, suddenly tore off in support. See what I mean? Any self-respecting All Black would have somehow made time in his busy schedule to give me a quick smack in the chops before leaving.

This mentality *Britannique*, as the French refer to it (usually with a groan), also showed through in other aspects of their game. Somewhere in their collective psyche it is obviously writ large in concrete that 'Thou shalt keep it simple, thou shalt keep it conventional'.

While the parameters of the conventional for the French stretch clear from one horizon to the other, for the Brits they go only about the width of the field. As long as the Falkland Islanders agreed to it, you could stake what remains of the British Empire on the Lions full-back kicking for the line when in possession of the ball behind his own 22m line. No attempts to do the unexpected. No quick put-ins to the line-out. No tricky penalty moves. Overall, no razzamatazz. Safe. Simple. Conventional. Even such relatively standard fare as dummy passes, chip kicks and switch attacks seemed entirely absent from their play. So, as the game went on we Australians learnt that the lines of the Lions' attack would come at us straight along the main highways, with no sorties out into the jungle, no tricky flanking movements, no snipers and no roving commando assaults. It was 'straight up the guts' as we say in the business. Not that it was boring, though. No sooner had we forwards set up satisfactory roadblocks to stop their highway advances, than the wretches would call in an air attack, invariably with bombers.

Once hard up against our immovable green barricade, captain Dean Richards would have the ball sent back to five-eighth Craig Chalmers, who would hoist the ball on high to come bombing down behind our main defensive lines. The retreat would then sound, and we forwards would have to hightail it back through the low country to form a new roadblock down-field, where the whole process would be repeated again.

But that wasn't the worst of it. The worst of it was their moral duplicity. Time and again, when we had finally managed to get the ball on our side of the maul we would discover a Lion, by now under the same muddy cloak as us, skulking around among us and trying to get the ball under the false pretences of being an Australian. Some of the guys were in favour of having the next Lion found

27

doing this shot on the spot as a fifth-columnist, but in the end calmer heads prevailed and we found a more moderate system.

For the last twenty minutes of the game no ball was passed in a maul unless the receiver could answer a question from the passer along the lines of 'How do you spell vegemite?' and 'What are Bob Hawke's middle names?'. Any time we heard 'Vege-what?' or 'Bob who?' in reply, we smashed 'em. That put paid to their little caper. But the Lions' larger caper, of playing hard, risk-free rugby very well, should be a lot more difficult to stop in coming weeks as they become progressively more match-hardened. Stay tuned.

GETTING OUR TEETH INTO THE TOULONNAIS

Brive-en-Limousin: Down here in this lost corner of France where the passion of the people runs to Rugby Union, there has been of late a new sound in the night air, mingling with the barking of dogs, the crowing of roosters and the haunting cry of a lost and lonely freight train whistling away in the distance. *'Krr-kr kr kr, krr-kr kr kr, krr-kr kr kr'* . . . It is at first hard to distinguish as it wafts back and forth with the breeze but gradually . . . gradually . . . it becomes clearer and, yes, it is, astoundingly, the sound of 50 000 pairs of teeth gnashing away in rhythmic harmony.

The cause of this eerie phenomenon? None other than the prospect of the mighty Toulon rugby team, champion of all France, arriving by plane to play a game against my own team of Club Athletique Briviste. The gnashing is in aggressive ecstasy at the thought of what we local lads are going to do to the uppity Toulonnais. Though this event is ostensibly a game, a fairer description probably would be a mini-war—from the Toulon side of things, at least.

My team mates and I are above that. We will be on nothing less than a crusade. A crusade for the honour of our whole region, which has been held in a blind trust down in Toulon since the last time we played them. *Krr-kr.* On that dim December day *Krr-kr*—Black Sunday it's known as—*Krr-kr*, they won—ahem—*Krr-kr*, 62–0.

Impossible to exaggerate the seriousness with which our defeat was viewed by the good burghers of Brive. It was not merely that we were sportsmen of the town's best-known club and that we had gone down in a more than ignominious defeat against the hated big-city boys of Toulon. It was that we were the town's chosen warriors, with all the glories and comforts that this privileged position warrants, and we had disgraced Brive and the Brivistes by not even lifting our swords to defend ourselves.

On our return to Brive the next day, I remember reflecting that never had the sporting-hero business looked so gloomy. But that's all behind us now. This time things are going to be different. They may have won in crushing style last time by rattling up a good half-century but this time, by God, it is our turn to bat.

How can we even presume the possibility of winning after suffering such a hideous defeat? Because this time the Toulonnais are going to be playing on our turf and, as this is in France, that makes all the difference. At three o'clock, when we Brivistes first pour out of the trenches to get into the hand-to-hand stuff with the Toulonnais, we will do so supremely confident of one thing.

This is that, while our supply lines of emotional will-to-win are absolutely secure, coming to us as they do as a palpable force from our own 12 000 supporters surrounding the battlefield, our opponents will be operating no less than 700km from their own base—drawing sustenance only from a bare scattering of supporters.

In such a hothouse emotional atmosphere, my team-mates and I, so timid at Toulon, will consider it a positive privilege to throw our bodies on to the ball in front of the whirling maelstrom of Toulonnais boots, a positive pleasure to tackle ourselves to exhaustion and beyond, and positive ecstasy to run all over anything that moves in a red jersey.

While the Toulonnais will hesitate that barest moment wondering if the effort is all worth it so far from home, we will storm ashore and swarm all over them before they know what has happened. That's why we'll win. That's why we'll moider da bums. That's why we are going to beat a team that only two-and-a-bit months ago atomised (read 'moleculised') us by 62 points. And that's why we are a very, very funny bunch of people, we French, now that I come to think of it.

PS And we did win. Nailed the brutes 4–3 for my single most memorable game in France.

CLAN WAR—WHY WE WON'T GET OFF SCOT FREE

Every international rugby team you play has a certain *feel*, unique to them.

With the All Blacks of old, it sometimes seemed you were up against a particularly humourless bunch of prisoners on day-leave from Long Bay, all of whom understood they would get a month reduced from their sentence for every brutal bruise they caused.

Against the Fijians on the other hand, the slightly carnival atmosphere shimmering over the play could give the impression you were playing against fifteen happy-go-lucky lads drawn from the beaches that very morning.

Scotland is altogether different again.

It starts when you hear the first strains of their magnificent national anthem coming at you through the mist, before the game begins. To the strain of bagpipes it goes:

> Oh flower of Scotland,
> When will we see your like again,
> That fought and died for,
> Your wee bit hill and glen,
> And stood against them,
> Proud Edward's army.
> And sent them homewards,
> To think again.

Perhaps it doesn't do the song justice to see it there in black and white instead of hearing it sung by fifteen steely-eyed Scots with steel-studded boots on, but for a wee footballer it is the moral equivalent of facing the haka in singing form. And it sets up the feeling you begin to have five minutes into the game . . .

As if, by some cosmic flash, we Emerging Wallabies had been transformed into fifteen McTavishes, doing battle on the moors with the men of the McDougall clan over some ancient and hideous wrong committed by our ancestors.

Somehow, the affable fellows we had been palling around with in Melbourne Airport on the way down from Sydney, the same ones we had then raced our buses with neck-and-neck over the Derwent River Bridge on the way to our separate Hobart hotels, somehow these lads were transformed into fifteen whirling dervishes who had something personal against us. We wretched McTavishes would be taught a lesson we would never forget, they seemed to be saying to us with every shuddering tackle. And that's not the worst of it.

The worst was when, 30 minutes into the game, we thought we had them tamed, thought we had given the McDougalls a good enough workover that they'd have something to gripe about for another three centuries or so. That's when they brought on the true leader of the McDougalls—the Scottish Test captain, David Sole, came on to the field as a replacement. Before our eyes the whole lot of them suddenly grew a good 30cm taller, put on ten kilos and all started working together for the first time.

At that point, we Emerging Wallabies had withstood the initial onslaught, and counterattacked, and were twenty points up. All to no avail. With Sole now leading them, the McDougalls were given new heart and purpose, and though some might point to second-half wind and the send-off of our prop Matt Ryan as significant factors in the Scots' remarkable comeback to a 24–all draw, others of us thought it was most importantly Sole's presence that made the difference.

Though the Scots had all been playing as if they had a personal grievance against us up to that point, none seemed more aggrieved than he. Was it Sole's own great-great-grandfather in a direct line who was done over by us McTavishes all those years ago?

We knew not. And frankly, it was all a fraction beyond our Australian ken. The Wallabies will do well to take their grievances out on the Scots, because the McDougalls will certainly be taking it out on them. And to send the proud Scots homewards, to think again, is going to take a mighty effort from the Waratahs.

TIME TO FACE THE ALL BLACK MUSIC

Ka mate! Ka mate!
Ka ora! Ka ora!
Tenei te tangata puhuruhuru
Nana nei i tiki mai
I whakawhite te ra!
Upane! Upane! Upane!
Ka upane! Whiti te ra!

The curious thing about facing the All Blacks in a haka before the game is that their eyes don't actually focus on anything. They're not staring at you, or through you, or even over your head to the homeland. Their eyes are just entirely glazed and unseeing, which is eerie.

Combine it with the fact that all the veins in their necks throb in unison as they yell at you at the top of their voices, while they're making all these ferocious hand movements besides, and it's almost overwhelming in effect. In reply, you almost want to yell *'Taxi!'* just to get the hell out of there. But there's nothing for it but to stand there and face the macabre music.

And it does not help even when, in a previous effort to demystify the haka, you happen to know a translation of it as roughly thus: *It is death! It is death! It is life! It is life! This is the hairy person, who caused the sun to shine! Abreast! Keep abreast! The rank! Hold fast! Into the sun that shines!*

The only part that really makes sense to me is the 'It is death! It is death!' part. Anyway, eventually the All Blacks stopped shouting, we stopped our knees from knocking together, and the game began.

The South Australian XV, bolstered by six of us ring-ins from interstate, up against the might of New Zealand.

We had one, and only one, advantage. That is, that while it was a tremendous honour for us to be playing against the All Blacks, the New Zealanders had the dubious honour of playing against a side which the All Blacks had pushed into *The Guinness Book of Records* previously by beating them 117–6.

So they took us lightly while we took them deadly seriously, and many of the South Australians played the game of their lives; which is surely why the match turned out as it did. Far from running riot against us, they managed only to cross our line five times in 80 minutes, for a final score of 48–18.

Not bad when you're up against a side that includes Steve McDowell, Ian Jones, Mike Brewer, Michael Jones, Zin-Zan Brooke, Vai'iga Tuigamala, Terry Wright, John Kirwan and Grant Fox. And despite such pedigree, two of the All Black tries were simple runaways, relying naught on construction, and two others were after I had been sent from the field and South Australia were thus down to only fourteen defenders.

Further, the All Blacks' adaptation to the new rules was 'not terrific'. They made no quick taps, took no quick throw-ins and tried nothing new under the new-rules sun.

In the past in such games, it was not uncommon to sight the ball only after an All Black had placed it between the posts, after the whole pack had mauled it all the way down field. But in this game, we were all surprised at how often we could get our hands on the ball and simply hold on for grim death until the referee, under the new rules, was obliged to award the scrum put-in to us.

Was this unexpected vulnerability of the All Blacks in this phase of play because they are caught betwixt and between as to the best sort of maul to pursue under the new rules? Maybe. Or maybe it was just a rare off-night for them. The latter is more likely, because they were also off their game in rucking. In past games against the All Blacks, my back has looked as if the brutes had been playing noughts and crosses on it with their boots. But after this game, there were just a few casual grazes.

Line-outs? Ian Jones was imperial in the middle as usual but we managed to snaffle a lot of ball up the back from them, as well as a lot from two-man line-outs. All in all, not a great performance from them, though probably an aberration. As for my getting sent off, for fighting and obstruction, gimme a break.

Of *course* I did everything possible to disrupt the flow of the All Blacks' ball from the maul. What else are you going to do, playing with South Australia against the mighty All Blacks, when you don't want to trouble *The Guinness Book of Records* people one more time? And of course they belted me for my trouble, and of course I belted them back. No problems there from either side, and no hard feelings.

That this then led to me being called out four times by the referee with four different All Blacks, no doubt gave the impression that I spent the whole night brawling, whereas, in fact, I only spent a minor part doing that, and all for a good cause—defending South Australian soil from the incursions of notoriously voracious raiders.

An odd room. Spacious, fluorescently lit, carpeted, a couple of windows, a few scattered bare benches. Nothing peculiar in that. Rather, it is the people in it and the situation we face which gives it such an unreal quality

Look over there—pttt, pttt, pttt—at the source of the only noise. It is Scottish full-back Gavin Hastings, passing a rugby ball back and forth to Martin Knoetze, the Springbok winger.

The two do it with grim, single-minded intensity as around them everyone else is lacing his boots, getting a final rub-down or shaking hands in an equally odd, sort of consolatory manner.

Though I know for a fact that everyone here has spent the last few nights singing loudly and rollicking around town together, we are now only ten minutes from a full-blown Test match. Against no less than the New Zealand All Blacks.

Though there has been a 'Barbarian' atmosphere in the last few days, the exigencies of playing the All Blacks allows no such lassitude as kick-off approaches. This is the third and final Test of the centenary series and, with the score at 1–1, the New Zealanders are deadly serious. Not that we expected anything less.

Pttt, pttt, pttt.

Suddenly, a knock on the door and a loud voice: 'Can we have the skipper to make the toss, please?'

No fewer than four faces look up instinctively. Wallaby captain Nick Farr-Jones; former All Black captain, Gary Whetton; the leader of the Scots, David Sole, and Western Samoa captain, Peter Fatialofa. If you have to go over the top of the trenches against the All Blacks, then these are good men to have beside you.

Farr-Jones is back from the toss and speaks for the first time. At moments like this, many captains are like steaming kettles of words, boiling over with random configurations of aggressive phrases, all of which are ultimately meaning-less.

The thrust of what they say is: 'Belt them, for they are vermin.' Farr-Jones is never like that. Now, as always, his instructions are as precise as his sentiments.

Each man must concentrate on fulfilling his task, he says, beating his opposite number, making things happen, and the scoreboard will take care of itself.

And do not forget the historic opportunity that beckons here—for there are perhaps twenty times more prime ministers and kings on this earth than people who can claim to have beaten the All Blacks in a rugby series. And *win*, he says, win for each other, if not for the 'World' we represent.

True enough. When Nick finishes speaking, there is a collective outlet of breath as everyone feels the immediate compulsion to get up and walk around. As the final seconds tick away, there is a lot of touching between the players—warm pats on the belly and back and yet more handshakes.

It is somehow an affirmation of unity before the coming battle. Then another knock on the door, and the players of the World XV file out, to sunlight, the crowd's roar, and the All Blacks.

I hate being a reserve. Though I would push a peanut up Main Street with my nose to be a reserve for this particular team, it is nevertheless incredibly frustrating. In fact, all there is to do is to do what all reserves do: wish an injury on your team-mates that will disable them long enough to get you on the field and into the game. You know you shouldn't think thus, but you do. At least I do.

I concentrate most of my hexs, spells and malicious wishes on the knees and ankles of Wallaby Troy Coker, who is playing in my spot in the second row, but through some cosmic mix-up, it is in fact Willie Ofahengaue who eventually succumbs. He has injured himself and must come off. So with ten minutes to go I am on against the All Blacks in a Test match.

But *these* can't be All Blacks. See. All Blacks are not born, they are quarried; they don't have faces, they have canvasses of skin on which scars, squashed noses and cauliflower ears are randomly attached.

And these guys don't look like that. Most of them look young and fresh-faced. They don't look intimidating at all. The recent All Black purges seem to have all but wiped out cauliflower ears and broken noses.

But the new guys still run and hit and ruck pretty much like All Blacks, for all that. The game is incredibly fast and physical. When, on one occasion, I fall into the whirling maelstrom of an All Black ruck, I know for sure that I'm in a real All Black Test match.

The game is over and we have lost. Damn, damn, double damn. The particularly galling thing is that we have lost to a team who though good, do not have the aura of invincibility of their predecessors. They may get that aura in time, but for the moment they are no more than a very good rugby team.

It is rising midnight at the reception after the game, and perhaps ten of us are standing around singing the Scottish national anthem, *Flower of Scotland*, led by Gavin Hastings and coach Ian McGeechan. We are giving it our all, for no other reason than that we loved it.

3 THE TOURS

TOURING WITH THE TRIBE I—FRANCE

In a hotel courtyard in Lille, in far northern France, a sombre group of Australians is gathered around Bob Templeton, tribal elder of the Wallabies.

'They shall not grow old, as we that are left grow old, age shall not weary them nor the years condemn . . .' recites Templeton amid the bowed heads, as curious curtains draw back around.

It is 11 am on 11 November. Some 50 kilometres south is the Somme Valley—where lies the largest collection of Australian war graves outside of Gallipoli. In four hours' time, half of this huddled group will go into battle against the French in the second Test.

Of course, this sporting skirmish will be trivial in comparison with the great massacres of the World Wars. And yet, without wishing to lay it on too thickly, there are parallels. Like the soldiers who left Sydney Harbour for France three-quarters of a century ago, the Wallabies have become comrades in arms nearing completion of what in many ways has been an almost military term of duty. Behind them lie six weeks of intense training, travelling and competing, wearing their country's colours across three continents. For six weeks, they have lived together, trained together, played together and fought together.

A collection of 30 individuals has been welded into the latest generation of a famous warrior tribe—with its own rituals, idiosyncrasies and exclusive warrior rules. To outsiders, some of these rites may appear anachronistic, shallow, even silly. Too bad. What the tribal elders have been doing is creating an insider ethos, making each player feel part of a team, and, more importantly, making them aware that they are inheritors of a long tradition.

It started far from France, on a Monday in early October when 30 of the best rugby players in the country, culled from the offices and backblocks of eastern Australia, gathered in a North Sydney hotel to be issued their kits and to put in three days of hard training before flying to Canada. An old rugby hand had said to me years before that in his considered opinion, rugby tours were 'the highest form of life on earth'. Even allowing for hyperbole, he wasn't far off the mark. What? Sweaty men torturing themselves is meant to be a high form of life? Damn right, but only because there's a lot more to it than mere rugby.

'One, two, three, four, *hit*! Back. One, two, three, four, *hit*!' In a little harbourside park at Cammeray, Wallaby coach Bob Dwyer is putting the squad through its paces on the tackle bags, as one after another, in military precision, we line up to punish these infernal plastic sacks of cotton. Of all the physical drills before departure, the tackle bag drill is by far the most exhausting. Not coincidentally, it is also the one we do most often.

'At least,' we console ourselves, 'they won't be able to take these heavy tackle bags to Canada and France.' Error. Three days later, we are appalled to see, while we are filing into the economy section of the jumbo jet bound for Canada, the same wretched tackle bags are receiving first-class treatment from Dwyer, Templeton and Andy Conway, the manager of the side.

We get the message: on this tour we are going to end up not just physically fit, but mentally toughened.

'So guys, these are the two packs I want to compete against each other in the line-outs . . .' Dwyer reads the names. 'Daly, Kearns, McKenzie . . .' It is a painful moment. For the first time, instead of being an integral 30, we have been divided, halved into two teams of fifteen. The selection process has begun. Suddenly team-mates have become rivals. It is obvious to us that one line of players is the provisional Test team; the other is likely to play only the mid-week games.

There are long faces in my pack. If the Test side were

picked tomorrow, we would be mere spectators. For the rest of the training, there is just a little bit of venom in our tackles. Refusing to acknowledge that we are in fact the B-Team, we call them the 'Bombers' just to spite them. Soon we have a name for ourselves: the 'Assassins'—the A-Team.

It is a piece of fun, but there is a serious side to it, too. Inexorably, the dotted line that is drawn down the middle of the squad at that training session becomes a little clearer and a little darker with each successive training session. Which is as it should be, from a rugby point of view—it is precisely this internal competition which will give us the steel to face the French when the real Test comes.

In Fudpuckers Hamburger Grill in Edmonton, Canada—on the first leg of the tour—four Wallabies knock back hamburgers and discuss the opening match played the day before. Three of us have never played a Test before—while one, the hooker Tom Lawton, is a veteran of no fewer than 41 of them over the last six years. I mention how moved I had been the day before, when we fifteen Wallabies had stood arm in arm before the match and sang the Australian national anthem for the first time on a foreign field.

Tom snorts. To our looks of surprise, he replies: 'Mate, I'll tell you what "moving" is. Moving will be if you play a Test match in France . . . and they play the Australian national anthem and the fifteen of you can only just hear the tune from the band against the voices of the 70 000 froggies that are screaming for your blood, but you all belt it out anyway . . . and you line up to receive the kick-off, and you can see this little sliver of white coming straight at you end over end like it's in slow motion and you take it, and get belted by four of them, but your mates close ranks to protect you and knock them backwards and you form the first scrum with your blood just trickling down your nose on to your lip and your eyebrow's swelling up and you can see the grass about three inches from your eyeballs and you feel this massive heave coming from behind you . . . and that . . . *that* is what "moving" is, mate.'

43

Throughout this whole magnificent speech (personally, I put it right up there with Lincoln's battlefield address at Gettysburg), and for perhaps ten seconds afterwards, we are totally silent. The unspoken thought is: 'Will we, too, know what all that is like?'

We're in a hotel in Toulouse. The day has been spent flying across Canada and the Atlantic. Most of the Wallabies are 'shot ducks' (as we say in the trade) and retire to bed early. Three of the Wallabies, though, are having a quiet drink in the hotel bar when they decide to investigate music coming from a nearby ballroom.

Voila! A full-blown wedding. Almost instantly, the groom recognises one of the players as a particularly well-known Wallaby and immediately finds a place at his table for the three Australians. On into the wild night they go until 5 am, knocking back Bollinger and battling jet lag and eventually drowning in sheer rollicking adrenalin. Between the Wallabies and the wedding party there has been almost a total lack of linguistic comprehension, but to hear them tell it, no one really noticed.

Tours are not just about tackle bags.

It is about two o'clock in the morning. Nick, Tom and I are in a miserably dark and gloomy back alley, looking for a nightclub that is rumoured to be in these parts. It is slightly spooky. For the last three hours we have been loudly solving all the world's problems in a nearby bar. It has just shut and we are staggering—only very slightly.

Suddenly, up ahead in the gloom we see three figures approaching. Enemy? Friend? Muggers? In this dark alley, in a foreign country, we close ranks marginally and keep moving forward, with muscles tensed, to meet our fate.

'Tom, mon ami!' a voice rings out.

It proves to be Pierre Berbizier, the French Rugby captain, with two of his friends. They too, are looking for the nightclub. Berbizier knows Tom well from their recent World XV tour of South Africa and shakes his hand effusively. Me too. We have played against each other many times in the French domestic competition over the past four years and have had a few drunken soirees together.

His reaction to Nick is interesting. Not only is Nick his opposing captain in the Test match due in a few weeks, but he will also be his most direct adversary of the match, as they both play half-back.

After the most perfunctory of all possible handshakes, Berbizier somehow manages to place his body in such a position that Nick is excluded from the emerging circle, while he talks dix-neuf to the dozen to Tom and me. It is a direct snub, and doesn't he know it. In the dim light, I can just see the expression on Nick's face which says, sort of deathly calm-like, 'Pierre, for this slight you will be buried.'

Never a truer word unspoken.

'Here are the room lists,' says one of the 'duty boys' as the bus pulls into Clermont-Ferrand. 'Lawton and Crowley in room 105, FitzSimons and Williams in room 107, Junee and . . .' There is a groan from the front of the bus as Ian Williams, a relentlessly neat (read ridiculously neat) and tidy winger from the Eastwood club in Sydney, realises he will be rooming with me over the next few days. He makes his displeasure known to the whole bus.

'But Ian,' I later tell him, 'I'm different now, I've changed, I swear it!' He threatens to divide the room with yellow insulating tape into two clear halves—never giving me or mine permission to cross into his half.

Foolishly, he eventually believes me, and by the next morning my dirty clothes have washed up on his shores, together with football boots, old socks, jockstraps and all sorts of filthy paraphernalia, as he sits marooned on the island that is his bed. 'Roomies' change at every stop and team management allocates the pairs based on some hidden psychological plan to form the unbreakable bonds that will forge a Test match victory.

Here are the room lists . . . FitzSimons and McKenzie room 256 . . . This time it is me who groans. Just before the Test team is to be announced for the First Test, I have been placed in a room with Ewen McKenzie. Not that I have anything personal against Ewen; it is just that he has been injured for the past week and cannot possibly play in the First Test.

Once again it seems that I am a 'shot duck' because the tradition is that Test players always room together before the match to feed off each other's building adrenalin. For the next four hours my miserable room allocation is coursing through my mind until the actual moment the Test team is announced.

When my name is eventually called out to partner Rod McCall in the second row, the world shifts into slow motion. Each syllable of my name comes as a separate sentence. I remember little of the next twenty minutes other than handshakes, congratulations and the tune from the Swan Lager ad 'They said you'd never . . .'

For all the joy felt by some of us though, there is great disappointment in others and we head off to training as studies in opposite extremes of emotions.

The start of the Test was just like Tom said it would be . . . the anthem, the little sliver of white coming slowly end over end, the blood trickling down the nose on to the lip, the whole shebang. Tom was right. It really was moving. At the end of the game, amazingly, we have won by the record breaking score of 32–15. No foreign team had beaten the French in France by such a margin since 1905.

When the referee blows his whistle to signal the end (as I write this, the hairs on the back of my neck are standing up) we jump, holler and hug. Five of us crab-walk together towards the back-rower from Quirindi, Dave Carter, who is standing alone and dazed with blood pouring from his brow. Then we were six.

Total uproar. It is the 'happy hour' after the Test. The happy hour is an institution after each Wallaby game. All the touring party gather in a closed room to partake in secret rites and rituals which it is totally forbidden for all non-Wallabies to know (sorry).

Suffice to say though, that when the plickathenny is donddaaded at the jinrok, wokos guys jik lok. And you think that was bad? You should have seen the dugt-dugt.

The French have a phrase for it—*mettre a l'agonie*—and it means, in the rugby context, putting so much pressure on your opponents that it is an agony for them—and scoring should naturally follow.

Sure enough, this is exactly what the French do to us for fifteen minutes in the second half of the Second Test. We tackle them red raw, but they just keep coming.

At half-time it had seemed so different. We had been leading 13–6 and had dreams of becoming the first team to whitewash the French on their soil. Suddenly they awaken and play absolutely brilliant rugby, driving constantly forward in wave after wave and never once making a mistake. It is, in fact, 'agony'.

Even now it is a mystery to me where they got the incredible energy in those minutes—while we are tackling to exhaustion—as well as the amazing concentration they needed to get it right. Even allowing for the soil of Mother France beneath their feet, which traditionally gives the French powers above and beyond mortal men, it is an impressive display.

By the time the storm is over, they are leading 25–13. A late try for us brings it to 25–19, but it is too little too late. The whistle blows.

Having explored the outer frontiers of joy last week, this time we've jumped back over the wall and patrol the edges of darkness and disappointment. We are at least a little comforted by the knowledge that we haven't actually 'blown it' so much as lost to a side that played absolutely superbly at the crucial time.

The final lunch of the final day of the tour we are in a restaurant in Paris. It is the last gathering of the tribe before we go our separate ways—some home to Australia, some to England and some to Italy to play in the off-season. After six weeks fighting countless battles with and against each other, we are nothing if not intimate. The final ritual is performed. The names of each of the tour party is put into a hat, and drawn out two at a time. On the clock, each of the two people whose names have been drawn out must talk about the other for no more than a minute. Amid shouts, cheers, jocular jeers and perhaps even the odd tear, the deed is done. The bus departs. The tribe disbands.

WE DELIVERED MORE THAN THE TELEGRAM

'Australians all let us rejoice . . . for we are young and free.' Tim Gavin, the lock of the team, starts absolutely belting it out, as we fifteen Australians stand in an all-embracing circle, ready to do battle in the first Test against the best that the haughty, the strutting Gauls can offer.

Something about Tim's passion for the anthem communicates itself to the rest of the Test team and from a merely enthusiastic rendition, we pass on to a lung-bursting and slightly crazy rendition, which makes up in volume what it lacks in harmony.

This is the beginning of Test rugby for me; the first time it feels really different from other important matches. We are not going to just 'win this one for junior' or for our club or state, for whoever or whatever, but rather this time, above all, we are playing for the very nation from which we have sprung.

Sure, it may sound like romanticised claptrap from the other side of the world, but for better or for worse, that is definitely the feeling among us. We are resolved to either win or to go down with all guns blazing.

Whatever it is, there is no doubt that the fifteen Australians before kick-off all have large lumps in their throats. The whistle blows and it is on. Five-eighth Michael Lynagh puts the ball right on the money, and if we don't actually recover the ball from the kick-off, we at least deliver a telegram to the French front door, saying that if they want to win the game, they will have to bleed for it. Macho crap? Absolutely. But we deliver the telegram all the same.

The first twenty minutes are strangely quiet. We cannot believe they are not throwing more at us. They cannot believe we are putting out all their flames before they turn into a bushfire. At half-time, France lead 12–10. While they may feel they have the game well in hand, we, on the contrary, feel they are ready to be nailed to the wall. And there is passionate discussion in the half-time huddle about how best to do this.

Winger Ian Williams effectively wins the discussion by putting the ball next to the posts, five minutes into the second half, after great Lynagh lead-up work, bringing the score to 16–12 in our favour. For the first time, the constant chatter coming from the French side of the maul about all the awful things they are going to do to the abysmal Australians starts to diminish as they contemplate the awful prospect of looking up at the cracks in the ceiling that night, wondering what on earth they did wrong.

Nick Farr-Jones, the captain, brings it into a huddle and says: 'This is it, guys, it's now or never, they will now throw everything at us and if we are going to win, we've got to tackle to the death and beyond.'

Sure enough, that is exactly what transpires and during the next ten minutes our shoulders are made red-raw after wave upon wave of French hurl against us. In the middle of it all, a try by David Campese brings us to 28–15, and neither we—nor the French—can quite believe it.

Only five minutes to go now. Once again they launch and once again we hold them and then score—the Campese goosestep and then Horan in the corner for his second try. The score was 32–15 to the team that was never meant to be, and a 'thanks for coming' for the French. If this is Test rugby, give me more of it.

TOURING WITH THE TRIBE II—NEW ZEALAND

Way back in 1975 when the British Lions team to New Zealand had completed their arduous six-week tour, the story goes that at the instant the jumbo left terra firma on the way back to the blessed home countries, there was an outbreak of spontaneous applause. New Zealand was behind them and falling further away all the time, God Save the Queen. Crank this kite up and let's get home.

Fifteen years on, that story was told to the 1990 Wallabies and raised not a single quizzical glance nor even a mildly surprised look. We understood perfectly. They just don't make tours tougher than this one.

In the array of possible rugby achievements for international teams, beating New Zealand in a Test series is right up there on the summit of Everest—and commensurate efforts are required. Sure, there'll be good times and bad times, as there are on every tour, but on no other tour are the hills so steep, the winds so cold, and the crevasses so potentially deep as they are on this one.

In early July, as a touring party of 35 players and officials, we set out for the distant mountain. Touchdown, Auckland Airport. If ever there was a testament to the powers of modern technology, this is it. Flying blind, the pilots managed to bring the plane right from the sunny skies of the lower stratosphere, down through the greatest rainstorm since Noah, right on to what we hope and pray is a runway.

This is not rain as in 'raining' or wind as in 'windy'—it is lash as in 'lashing' and scream as in 'screaming'. While starkly impressive to us at the time, by the end of the tour a storm like this would occasion little comment. Only, like Pavlov's dogs, we start to look for our boots, because if there is wind and rain outside, it's a sure bet that training must be soon. Bewdy. Lemme at that mud. Welcome to New Zealand.

51

And so it's north to the town of Hamilton in the province of Waikato. Whatever else you may say about New Zealand, it surely has some of the most spectacular scenery on earth, and even those small parts of it that have been developed retain the 'Approved by Mother Nature' logo pressed upon them with a green stamp.

The Waikato team are known locally as the 'Mooloos'—presumably a reference to the importance of cows to the economy—and the traditional method for encouraging the team is to ring cow bells (without a word of a lie) throughout the game.

As the countdown to the kick-off moves into bare minutes, the packed crowd becomes increasingly restless with delicious expectation. Three minutes, two minutes, one minute . . . and counting. With the whistle to start the game, the crowd lets out a collective, satisfied 'oomph!' and happily settles down to watch.

In New Zealand, where rugby is as much a part of the blood as white and red cells, the crowds don't seem to simply watch games so much as *feed* off them. Ergo, the kind of half-starved look in the eyes of the Waikato crowd before the game fades at the end into a sort of glazed, well-fed look. They are happy, as their team has won and won well. Our team has lost one that we probably should have won. Dammit.

We've lost Bobby. The news is disastrous. In the first half of the game against Auckland, Brendan (Bobby) Nasser, the breakaway who comes to the Wallabies from a dentistry practice in Queensland, has fractured his cheekbone.

Preliminary diagnosis is that the damage is such that he will have to almost immediately return to Brisbane for an operation. This news hits hard, partly because we have lost a good warrior for the coming crucial battles and partly because we are conscious that a good part of the Wallabies' collective soul resides in his gentle breast.

At a team meeting at the hotel, Bobby, back from the hospital and with an icepack on his cheek, manages to get out a few choked words wishing us well for the rest of the trip. If we were feeling lowly before, we feel positively wretched now. As I recall, no one in the room actually sheds tears, but there is no doubt that if all those 'lumps in the throats' were to be stacked end on end, there would have definitely been five out and out bawlers.

Scrum training. The wind and mud and rain. A godforsaken field on the west coast of the South Island. 'Fitzy, your back isn't straight, your feet are too far back and you're absolutely ruining our scrum,' forwards coach Bob Templeton is screaming at me through the gale.

This piece of information comes as no surprise to me. There is something about some guys which makes them excellent captains . . . and about others which makes them destined to weave their way through opposing backlines. Unfortunately, there is something about yours truly which makes coaches love to pick on me whenever it comes to scrum training.

Ever since as a little boy, I pulled on a pair of boots, it has always been my lot to accept full blame for the scrum whenever anything goes wrong. That is my cross and I bear it with as much grace as I can under the circumstances. But it is hard.

On this occasion, Tempo has deemed we need another good half-hour of scrum training in an attempt to get it (and most particularly me) right. The mud below, the grey above, the wind behind, my head strangled between two sets of incredibly muddy and gritty thighs—why, oh why couldn't I have been a cricketer? They never have to go through this hell.

The morning of the First Test breaks over the Australians gathered in the trenches. For those playing, there is mixed in with all other thoughts a very acute awareness of just how long it is until the battle commences. 'In just five hours and 40 minutes, I'll be out there.' 'Eighty minutes of play, only 80 minutes. Make each one count.' 'Hit ! Hit ! Hit !' 'Scrums: I *gotta* get my shoulder right on his hammer.'

'Aggression, aggression, *aggression*.' 'Whaddya mean you're feeling tense? This is absolute child's play compared to Gallipoli. Think of that and give it everything. Five hours 23 minutes to go. . .'

Playing Test matches is a big deal. Playing Test matches against the All Blacks is, to give them their due, the biggest deal of all. Even when you feel you are holding three or four aces, it is still a big deal.

Of the game, I now remember perhaps only two minutes of the eighty. A first scrum, where it felt as if an errant bulldozer had wandered into their pack—but our scrum holds. A kick-off where I am able to get a good hit on the All Black captain Gary Whetton. A barely missed tackle from which they score immediately.

And Kieran Crowley, the All Black full-back, running after our captain Nick Farr Jones, yelling: 'Mate! Mate! Mate! Pass me the ball, mate.' It's the old impersonate-an-Australian-on-the-field-by-yelling- 'Mate'-at-him-over-his-shoulder-and-hope-he'll-pass-you-the-ball trick. Nick was too smart by half. Ultimately, I remember defeat. You guessed it again: it tasted bitter.

Bubba is running up the snowy mountain in three-metre 'moon hops', as on the deck Wallabies are collapsing in fits of laughter. We are at the ski resort at the top of Mount Hutt the day after the First Test and just what is needed has occurred—something so hilarious that, for seconds at a time, the misery of defeat is forgotten.

Undeterred by our lack of skiing equipment, 'Bubba', aka Matt Ryan, our slightly rotund prop, puts a shovel over one shoulder and the handle attached to the bunny ski rope between his thighs and trundles off up the mountain. It is pure comic genius, reaching even greater heights when he eventually reappears, roaring down the mountain on his shovel and riding that nag until it drops. Definitely one of those 'you had to be there' stories, but 'twas something to see.

Dropped. For the Second Test, myself and four others have been omitted from the line-up in an effort to come up with a solution to the growing All Black problem. We are all suitably devastated and stagger singly off to our rooms to stare at the walls for a while and, with pure black malice, call the wrath of the rugby gods down on those who have done us down.

'Hear me oh great Thor, for I beseech thee/May the mud of New Zealand swallow them whole/May the goalposts fall upon them/May they never be allowed to forget the venal sins they have visited upon me this day.'

This sort of routine works well in solitude, but after half an hour or so we know we need to pool our venom to properly maintain the rage—it is time for the Tearing Down Ceremony.

The TDC is something of an institution on all international tours; those that have been dropped for Test matches get together in private (all of the so-called Test players are banned) and proceed to tear down anything and everything involved even remotely with their demise.

This particular TDC is a great success. It is cathartic—even as the rage builds, it is being released, and by the following morning you can almost bring yourself to choke out 'good morning' to one of the selectors. Almost, but not quite. The ingrates.

Trouble is, we lose the Second Test. Gloom. Doom. Seemingly.

'Come quickly, you gotta see this!' Paul Carozza, the Wallaby winger (and my room-mate for the New Plymouth leg of the tour), has burst into the room to give me news from 'the front' at the hotel bar. For what is known locally as the 'Dance of the Desperates', the bar has been overtaken by the monthly meeting of the local mature-age singles club, and a small pocket of Wallabies in the corner is manfully resisting the continued assaults of all and sundry.

We send out for reinforcements and by close to midnight have managed to secure all the forward posts well enough to soak up the scene. With the jukebox blaring, the moose head shaking on the wall, the well-oiled singles dancing up a storm and bouncing from wall to wall—it is a marvellous slice of life to have happened upon. We carouse till closing time, early training be damned.

In the game against Bay of Plenty, there is among us a strong body of opinion we have indeed copped plenty and that, in fact, in so doing, our opposition has gone well beyond the allowable amount of assault and battery.

In what was to be the only real brawling and foul play of the tour, we lose Bubba Ryan with a deep gash in his head, and Bobby Nasser, who had unexpectedly rejoined us from Brisbane, again is forced to depart the field, this time with a long cut along his eyelid.

On a field of slush, in rain and wind, we have been ambushed, bushwhacked, hung down, brung down, strung down—and Bay of Plenty emerges unexpectedly victorious. Violence aside, Bay of Plenty is a superbly committed team and it is a salutary lesson to us that, in New Zealand, even anonymous teams are capable of knocking you over. But we are about to give a lesson of our own . . .

Going into the Third Test, the chips are, as they say, down. We have lost the first two Tests and if we lose the last we will be the first Australian team since 1972 to have been whitewashed by the Blacks. But we nailed them. When the final whistle blows, we have won by 21–9 and are the first team to beat the mighty All Blacks in the last four years. And unlike the French in Nantes in 1986, we have done it without resorting to untoward tactics of violence. It was fair and square, without even accusations against the referee, so . . . thanks for coming.

The outpouring of joy on the field snowballs through the tunnel, gathering the non-Test players as it goes, bursts through the door and explodes in the confined space of the dressing room. War cries, champagne, the national anthem, the requisite pounding of backs and much hugging.

The victory is all the sweeter because, like all great victories, it was against the odds and unexpected by the outside world. We didn't scale the summit of Everest by winning the series, but nor did we fall into the deep crevasse so many had predicted.

The All Blacks, for their part, are gloomy and chastened, but sincere in their congratulations. This tour was marked by the unusually cordial relations between the two teams and every cliché there ever was about the camaraderie of opponents after the battle is fulfilled that night at the Test dinner. Later, en masse, the two teams hit the Arena nightclub in Wellington and on into the wild night they go. At dawn, our Queensland brothers must up stumps and catch a plane back to Brisbane. The tour is over. Auld lang syne.

A LITTLE GREEN . . . BUT MATURING WELL

Dunedin: And so ends another day in the life of the Wallaby tourist in New Zealand. Taking leave of team-mates in the bar below, he climbs wearily up the stairs to his room, as nearby church bells ring the midnight hour.

'Creak,' go the stairs. 'Bing-bong,' go the bells. 'Gee my back hurts,' goes his head.

Creak, bing-bong. How can so much pain fit into one little ankle? Creak, bing-bong. All that coffee is going to keep me awake musing half the night.

Sure enough.

The tour so far has been good, but not great.

Like fine wines, each rugby tour has a different texture, character and flavour. Though the vintage of the Wallaby tour to New Zealand 1990 has not yet fully matured, at this stage there is no doubt it is going to be a far stronger drop than the late '89 Canada–France vintage, for example.

To date the texture is rough and a little muddy; the character way less exotic and far more familiar (as if Australia were just over yonder mountain range); and the flavour at the moment, frankly, is a little acidic, though still very palatable.

All the Wallabies are agreed that what this particular 1990 vintage needs, at all possible speed, is the sweetness of a few more victories—particularly Test victories.

We are working on that, but the grapes don't crush easily in these parts. In fact, in the first Test last Saturday it felt less like an ordinary grape under our feet than a mid-sized boulder . . . but that's another story. Whatever, all metaphors aside, if we were all working very hard at training in the first two weeks of this tour, we are working with even more resolve now.

When I get back from this tour, if I never see another scrum machine again it will probably be still too late to reverse the permanent psychological damage I have suffered at the hands of those infernal contraptions. (Incidentally, it is as well the Australian press contingent turned up to training with paper bags on their heads earlier this week, and so escaped recognition, as the original plan had been to use them as scrum fodder, just for delicious variety.)

Outside of rugby though, the pleasures of touring in New Zealand are many and we have received very warm welcomes wherever we have gone, bar those wild jungle patches called rugby fields, where the natives have been as desperately inhospitable as ever I have seen. (What is it with those guys anyway?)

One of the amazing things about touring with the Wallabies in New Zealand is the extraordinary amount of adulation you receive whenever you are recognised, which is frequent. No, we Wallabies will never be treated as demi-gods, as are the All Blacks, but we don't do a bad little line as minor deities.

Why, what about what happened to me only the other night at a restaurant in Christchurch? No sooner had I entered the restaurant than everybody was staring and pointing at me, whispering behind their hands and winking and smiling at me in such a friendly fashion that I was almost overcome with gratitude. This went on all through dinner—I was the centre of attention in a crowded restaurant, but my fellow diners were in such awe of me they didn't dare approach, no matter how enthusiastically I waved and winked back. I felt magnanimously important, I thought they deserved a few handshakes and autographs, but they proved too shy.

Sure, there'll be folks back home who won't believe me, and will doubt that such hero-worship could happen to a footballer like me, but just ask David Campese or Nick Farr-Jones—they were right by my side the whole time. . .

DON'T WORRY ABOUT THE SCOREBOARD AND DON'T MENTION THE WAR

So that was Argentina. Some country. Around international Rugby traps the land of Los Pumas is regarded as something of an El Dorado for touring teams—the Promised Land. Rightly so.

The standard of rugby might not be quite as high as in France, there might not be the same sporting joy in beating Argentinians as in beating the English, but neither of those countries comes close to matching Argentina for sheer colour. Seen through the prism of a rugby tour, Argentina is nothing if not kaleidoscopic.

For what it's worth, here are a few scenes from the New South Wales rugby team's sojourn to Argentinian shores.

The bus pulls into the northern Argentinian town of Rosario after a five-hour drive from Buenos Aires and a fifteen-hour flight from Australia before that. We gain our hotel rooms with no little relief. (Wide-angled shot from outside Imperio Hotel, Rosario, in the semi-darkness.) 'Goodnight Jon-Boy. Goodnight Mary-Ellen. Goodnight Nick. Goodnight Rod. Goodnight Simon.' (Incredibly small passage of time, followed by the sound of a rooster crowing and . . .) 'Good morning *all*! Time for *training*!' The tone of the tour has been set—training is to be the one constant in our lives, even as the scene around us is ever-changing.

What is wrong with these guys? Don't they know when they are badly beaten? With five minutes to go in the game against Rosario XV, we Waratahs are a full twenty points ahead. The decent, gentlemanly thing for them to do now would be to put up an 'Out to Lunch' sign so as to let both sides peacefully coast home. But no-o-o. That would be too easy. These wretches *insist* on attacking relentlessly, running everything and playing for all the world as if they

60

were only a point behind and could still win the game; we are obliged to attack back and end up exchanging tries with them to win 34–12.

We met her at about 2 am in one of the more run-down sections of Rosario. When her flatmate let us in, Constanza, nineteen, was studying for her economics exams in a few days' time, but willingly put away her books to talk to two Australians. For half an hour she let us have it. Argentina's history from her perspective; its problems, how a country once so rich could now be so poor. The way she told it, the whole country was only saved from going down the gurgle-hole of history because the national plumbing system was one of the first parts of the infrastructure to go. Then she told us what she personally was going to do to set it right when she came to power in the year 2015 or so. Eva Peron move over . . . and what a good thing there is so much more to rugby tours than mere rugby.

It is in the dressing-room before the night game against the notorious Tucuman team. It is the sort of dressing-room that, given a sledgehammer and half an hour, you'd still be hard put to do $3.50 worth of damage to, as everything but *everything* is reinforced concrete.

Outside, the chants of Los Tucumanos—the 15 000-strong crowd reverberates their way into our little concrete bunker where captain Nick Farr-Jones is giving his final pre-match talk.

The basic theme he chooses is this: 'We are a long way from home, against a very difficult opponent, which will have the crowd totally with them, and the referee is their sixteenth man. To prevail, each of you must concentrate on performing your task and getting the better of your opponent. Don't worry about the scoreboard. If all fifteen of us just concentrate on our own task then the scoreboard will take care of itself.' (This speech was absorbed more or less—on average every player had a stand-off with his opposite number and the final score was 15–15.)

Perhaps two seconds after gaining our hotel room in Buenos Aires, my room-mate Tim Gavin turns the television on. If he hadn't, I would have. It's not that either of us are particularly Argentinian TV freaks—it's just one of the immutable rituals performed by all football teams upon entering their hotel rooms. Neither of us actually watch the TV—it's just an extra window in the room with changing, talking, scenery.

There is something about rugby coaches which invariably makes them think that their charges should operate under different rules from the rest of the populace. What other species of human would, after spending virtually the whole day travelling from Tucuman in the north to Mendoza in the south, be then obliged to don their kit and run around the local park, running into each other like demented rabbits, to the bemusement of the locals? Who else but we rugby players at the insistence of coach Rod McQueen?

When the session is over, we poor, bedraggled, benighted lot drag our weary way back through the park and happen upon a gaggle of twelve-year-old street kids playing soccer—using broken bricks as goalposts. A minute later, it is on. A full-blown soccer game between us and the kids. The sad fact is they have it all over us brute rugby players for skill, speed, and, particularly, *flair*. Twenty minutes in, we somehow manage to finally score a lone goal and—following America's lead in Vietnam—we declare victory and leave.

Back in 1932, D.H. Lawrence wrote to a friend in England: 'The Spanish wine, my God it is foul, cat-piss is champagne compared, this is the sulphureous urination of some aged horse.'

The Argentinians obviously did not learn the art of wine-making from their Spanish blood brothers—or at least they have refined it since. To any palate this is good stuff and a long way from being mere plonk. And it comes to us courtesy of one of the rugby clubs in the wine-making region of Mendoza. For an afternoon, the Waratahs have been their guests at one of the many barbecues we would attend on tour—drinking their wine, eating their impossibly thick steaks and accepting their hospitality. They have never seen any of us before and will likely never see any of us again, but as card-carrying members of the world-wide rugby fraternity, we qualify for their kindness.

Odd, the places rugby takes you. On the flight home, we first head directly south along the Argentinian coastline and, after three hours, stop to refuel at the southern outpost of Rio Gallegos. Throughout the tour so far we have been very careful not to talk about the F-A-L-K-L-A-N-D-S. (Don't mention the war, okay?)

But now, as it happens, we are at what was a staging post for the Argentinian assault on the Falklands/Malvinas off the coast from here. Now, we are *doubly* careful. But really there is no need. In all of Argentina the only aggression we have encountered has been on the rugby field and that has been tempered by great friendliness later. Other than that, it has been unremitting hospitality and we fly out with no little regret.

4 WORLD CUP WRAP

UP THROUGH AUSSIE EYES

It's on again, the biggest event in Rugby Union—the World Cup. The national teams from sixteen countries gather in the home countries and France for a four-group round-robin tournament for the right to a place in the final.

Not only bearing their countries' hopes in the contest, the teams will also be showing their national spirit, expressed in the way they play the game. And rugby, more than most endeavours, most effectively displays the national spirit. From the creative flair and derring-do of the French, to the dour grittiness of the New Zealanders, from the happy-go-lucky play of the Fijians to the technically excellent precision play of the Japanese, rugby as it has evolved in all its separate styles, is on display in this contest.

A look then at the contenders, their styles, their backgrounds, and their chances of winning World Cup II . . .

The British

Now let's be fair, if your land invents a sport, then of course it is only right and proper that you should dominate it internationally for at least the first century or so of its existence. The Brits did that in tennis, golf, bowls, badminton, sailing and just about every other sport you can think of including, to a degree, rugby.

And of course we don't begrudge them that first century of domination. But why, then, do they begrudge it to us when, as always happens, we take to the games they invented with such enthusiasm that we finish up peeing on them from a very great height in every sporting contest we find them? Why can't they just accept this as pretty much normal and be done with it, instead of always whingeing and claiming, as they do, that sometime real soon they're going to get their act together and then the rest of us had better look out!

Anyway, the bottom line is that while the British teams might have dominated Rugby Union at one time, those halcyon days have for the most part gone the way of the rest of the empire—into the realms of nostalgia.

While there are stylistic variations in the play of the home countries, they are basically variations on a theme, products of what the French scathingly refer to as the *mentalité Anglo-Saxonne*. For the forwards, concentration is fixed above all the set pieces of scrums and line-outs, while for the backs it's stolid, steady-as-she goes (two degrees to port, if you please Mr Briggs) orthodox play.

England

A few years ago it wasn't going too far to say that if William Webb Ellis, generally regarded as rugby's founding father, were alive today, he just might get a spot on the English team. These days though, he'd be doing it a bit tougher. Long the sleeping giant of European rugby, three years ago England awoke, just barely. Last year they stirred themselves . . . and this year they stood up for the first time in over a decade. They won the Grand Slam, beating all the other Five Nations teams, which is not a bad credential in anyone's language when you are going for a World Cup win. Despite their current status as possible world beaters though, it's instructive to note that the wretches haven't actually taken on the nominal best in the world for the past seven years.

One of the mysteries of the international fixture is why England have not toured New Zealand since 1985 and the All Blacks have not played a Test at Twickenham since 1983. It's almost as if the English managers have kept their precious fighter away from the real hard hitters for fear that he might be battered out of the ring. Terrific for the stats maybe, but a real problem when England find themselves up against the All Blacks in the World Cup, particularly after its recent 40–15 drubbing by Australia.

68

Wales

How the mighty have fallen. In the days of yore—about one and a half yonks ago, I think it was—Wales had the most feared pack of forwards in captivity, not to mention backs of genuine genius.

Wales were firmly atop the Everest of world rugby and to beat them at Cardiff Arms Park was considered a victory of truly America's Cup proportions. These days it is regarded, not to put too fine a point on it, as a win of Scrabble proportions or maybe Monopoly—no big deal at all.

The fact is the Welsh team has been so soundly raped and pillaged by Rugby League troops over the past few years that there is almost no virginity or booty left to take. Anytime anyone with talent shows his head, he is immediately offered a Rugby League contract, and before you can shout 'Taxi!', he is gone.

The Welsh will do it tough this World Cup. As tough as they used to be.

Scotland

Therein lies something of a mystery. By all numerical reckoning, with their small number of players to choose from (only some 13 000 as against England's 200 000), the Scots should have long been the doormats of the Five Nations competition. The doormats? Hell, they should have been happy to get even that far up off the ground. But somehow they never have been. There is something within Scottish spirit which has never allowed them to be humiliated in international rugby. They'll be beaten certainly, but only after a terrible price has been paid by their opponents.

And they came very close to beating the All Blacks as recently as last year, which is important—because it is all but certain that the winners of the Cup this year will have to step over the All Blacks' dead body to get there.

Ireland

Your guess is as good as mine. The Irish have made a habit in recent years of confounding all the pundits—zag-zigging way up and down from year to year when it was predicted that they would zig-zag. As witness, after winning the Five Nations in 1985 they were completely whitewashed in 1986, not winning a single game. In 1986 they were meant to be bad and were good. In 1990 they were meant to be good and were bad. This year they're meant to be bad so, like I say, it's anybody's guess how they'll go, but at least for them the portents are good.

For all their unpredictability in results, however, the Irish nevertheless enjoy the reputation of always playing attractive and stylish rugby. Like the Scots, they play with a great spirit that belies their numerical weakness, and they are particularly dangerous in Dublin, where their early matches are to be played.

France

What is there to say about the Frogs? Man for man, kilo for kilo, eyelash for eyelash, they are, for my money, the most talented side that will attend the Cup. But as we all know, talent alone does not win matches.

It is talent with sting, with guile, with strength, with organisation, with will-to-win that wins matches, and over the past few years, for various reasons, the French stocks have been down, way down, in these other areas.

Why? Because of a virtual civil war that has been going on between two strands of the French character.

The first strand is the famous French flair. This has not only allowed them to lead the world in fashion, food, love and all things creative, but also has allowed them to play rugby in superlative fashion with superb intuition, instinct and verve . . . a rugby that can't be coached but can only be nurtured.

The second strand is their passion for technology and all things modern. That is why they're the most computerised nation in Europe with the best roads, the best trains, telephone systems, etc. They live it.

For years French rugby was firmly in the flair trough and they did extremely well, albeit a little erratically. Then coach Jacques Fouroux tried to put them in the technological trough, by training them hard, endlessly analysing their play and endlessly trying to structure it à la the All Blacks. As I said, civil war resulted with one half of French rugby thinking it was a good thing and the other half screaming blue murder.

Fouroux in the end was metaphorically executed and new coach Daniel Dubroca has tried to take them back to flair, but it seems sure that, still a bit betwixt and between, the French are in no shape to wrest the Cup.

United States

If raw physical power and athletic prowess were the only things that won rugby matches, then the Americans would be a good chance to win the World Cup. With the team made up, for the most part, of ex-gridiron players there is no question that they have the physical means to do well.

Frankly, when I lined up against them in a test match in Brisbane last year, I nearly keeled over at the sight. They are big, big boys. However, what they have in physical prowess, they lack in experience and technique. No matter that they have line-backer ginormous forwards—and backs who can do the hundred in even time—when push comes to shove, it will almost certainly be those countries that know the correct technique for pushing and shoving that will emerge victorious.

Thus, for all their characteristic American enthusiasm and aggression, in this, a dinkum world series, where other countries are also allowed to compete, the buck of American world domination in all things great and small will surely stop here.

Canada

Though no doubt inheritors of a proud sporting tradition, the unfortunate fact is that most of the modern athletic talents of the Canadian people have been channelled into a single ice-hockey player by the name of Wayne Gretzky— more or less the greatest sportsman who ever walked the earth, the way the Canadians tell it. Ergo, there is very little talent left to go around the rest of the populous, and most of that has gone into sports other than rugby.

71

That said, Canada are not without their arguments and they are at least generally considered better than the Americans whom they regularly beat in their annual cross-border tests.

When the Wallabies played two Canadian teams on their way to France at the end of 1989, the local boys were particularly notable for the ferocity of their forward rushes. I personally got in the way of one of them, near our try line, and some mornings, when the light is just right, I can still make out the outline of the stampeding footprints as they trace their way up my body.

Japan

The Japanese have taken to rugby with surprising alacrity and in the past decade have emerged as a rising force on the international scene. What the French have in pure talent, the Japanese have in technique. Superbly drilled in all technical aspects of the game, their main problem is that they're fighting a war with simple rifles while most of the other teams have cannons.

Though the Hollywood war image of little men scurrying around hither and thither is obviously overdone, there is nonetheless truth in the fact that they are a people of diminutive stature. The rule of thumb for Japanese backs and forwards in international matches is that though they may run around their opponents they will almost certainly never run over them. Thus limited in their available courses of action, they start every test a little behind the eight ball, as it were.

The fat lady hasn't actually sung yet though, because, with famed Japanese industriousness, they have applied themselves to working out a system of play to overcome their physical deficiencies: perfectly executed ankle tackles to bring down the big 'uns, lots of two-man line-outs and a purity of form in scrum technique that would make many a frustrated coach weep with joy.

Romania

When the Romanian revolution broke out at the beginning

of last year, the very first person shot and killed was the captain of the Romanian Test rugby team, Florica Murariu—not because he was the captain or anything, but just because he was a soldier on duty who happened to be in the way when one of the first riotous citizens exploded into action.

A tragedy—but starkly symbolic of the problems that can beset a team behind the Iron Curtain, or what's now left of it.

Perhaps reflecting such rigours, the play of the Romanians is characterised by its robust and aggressive nature. While finesse may not be their strong point and one may learn little about the fine points of technique by watching them play, their boots 'n' all style has held them in good stead in recent years as they have from time to time scored impressive victories over such first-class rugby nations as Wales, France and Scotland.

But the effect of the revolution being what it is, they will be close to being the World Cup easybeats this year.

New Zealand

They're good. In fact, they're great. But they're not unbeatable, as the Wallabies' recent wins indicate. At the start of last year's Wellington game, the All Blacks looked as awesome as ever—replete with that special aura that seems to hang around them whenever they take the field. They didn't finish with that aura though . . .

The Wallabies tackled till their shoulders were red-raw, and anybody in a black jersey was pounded on even the suspicion that he might be about to do something with the ball.

The bottom line of this super physical approach by the Wallabies was that fifteen Kiwi players started the match looking like All Blacks, but ended looking only like fifteen bedraggled guys in black jerseys.

After recent defeats it will take some time for them to regain that aura of invincibility in the eyes of the Wallabies—who are the most 'winningest' team in the world against them.

73

But, like I said, the All Blacks are good for all that. In style, the forwards frequently look and feel like a giant black multi-Adidased (or Mizunoed, these days) centipede rampaging around the field, while in the backs for sheer toughness let alone speed, agility, etc., they are almost without peer. Almost.

Zimbabwe

Many moons ago, while hitching along a lonely road in the northern stretches of Shonaland Zimbabwe, my attention was diverted by what looked like a rugby game, sounded like a rugby game, smelt like a rugby game and . . . and . . . and . . . be damned if it wasn't a rugby game! And a first division one at that.

While expressing surprise that—after hundreds of kilometres of elephant herds, occasional lions and lonely, lonely farmhouses—I should stumble across a full colours encounter, I was icily informed by a tweed coat with an Oxbridge accent that 'though rugger in Rhodesia has been bled white by the political events of the 1970's, we intend to carry on regardless'.

And carry on they have indeed. Though most of the country's experienced talent flowed across the border to South Africa, rather than face up to black rule, they have recovered to the point where the game is now flourishing as never before. Not only have many of the whites returned after finding out Armageddon has failed to materialise but the gradual realisation has also begun to sink in that the other 97 per cent of the population can also run, kick and carry the ball . . .

If the trend of increased black participation continues, who knows who might win the World Cup in 1999.

For the moment, though, I think we're still safe, and in this World Cup the best Zimbabwe can hope for is to beat some of the smaller rugby nations, while serving as sparring partner for some of the bigger guns.

Their style, as near as I can discern from clippings, crackly phone calls and scraps of memory, is that of a poor man's Springbok team. Aggressive forwards act as the power of the throne with emphasis on the set pieces of scrums and line-outs—while woe betide the back who, through some tom-foolish idea, tries a trick or two and loses the ball.

Italy

Ah, the Italians. One could write a book on the interesting background of the game in Italy and the select spot it occupies (top shelf, left-hand corner) in the Italian sporting psyche. Introduced in the early part of this century, it made little headway until that well-known hooker, Benito Mussolini, seized upon it as a good way of toughening up the Italian people, and promoted it accordingly.

It is now enthusiastically embraced by a limited section of the population (mostly small and medium-sized towns in the north) while the rest of the populace, though often showing an admiring interest, maintains its passion for soccer.

The closest sister to Italian rugby in terms of style of play and approach is, not surprisingly, France, but what a beastly and overbearing sister she has been. In 55 odd years of international encounters (often the French B team does the honours) the Italians have not had a single solitary win—and if you think that's upsetting you should hear how the Italians feel about it.

As one who has played long and hard in both Italy and France, perhaps I can put forward this theory. The difference between Italian and French rugby is the difference between a rose with thorns and a rose without. Both have the beautiful blooming movements, the extravagant gestures, the marvellous colours. But only French rugby couples that with the sting of the thorn to prevent opposing teams crushing the life out of them. For one reason or another, the Italians have never been able to develop the requisite 'sting' to successfully compete at international level. Terrific to have them on board for the World Cup, for their colour and passion, but they will be unlikely to need to book another first-class seat on the way back to Rome in order to take the World Cup home with them.

Western Samoa and Fiji

In their approach to the game our Pacific Island brothers are the spiritual equivalent of the French and the Argentinians—'mighty little science but a mighty lot of dash'. Whatever the position on the field may be, whatever the score, the prevailing policy is full speed ahead, the ball must go through! Usually the ball passes through as many pairs of hands as possible as they all fall over themselves to get a touch of it.

The odd thing is that such an energetic brand of rugby should have evolved in tropical islands where the weather is nearly always so humid and hot. One would have thought that a more docile brand of rugby would be best suited to getting comfortably through the 80 minutes, but these lads habitually pound round the terrain as if there were Olympic sprint selectors in the stands. More than one opposing captain has profited from rare moments of calm to check that there really are only fifteen of the beggars.

The result of all their leg work and support play, though, is that their game is characteristically razzle-dazzle spectacular, and, though it's not always high-percentage rugby in terms of winning, if the ball bounces their way they are both capable of good results against the best in the world.

There's little to pick between the two, in terms of the aforementioned style, but Western Samoa are generally considered to be marginally superior. Both sides have tremendous passion for the game and, when playing them, one has the sense that they always hear the final whistle with genuine disappointment.

Argentina

A word before the beginning . . . for rugby players a rugby tour is a lot like sex—when it's good it's great, and when it's bad . . . it's still pretty good. Tours to Argentina are always great—the greatest destination a rugby team can hope for. In all seriousness, fair dinkum, no kidding, no joking, honest injun: Argentina is our answer to Mecca. Not only do the colours of life there run particularly rich and exotic, not only do your dollars or pounds or francs or whatever go a particularly long way, but the hospitality of the people is overwhelming all over the land, bar that 50 x 100-metre rectangle that they call the rugby field.

There, there is no hospitality whatsoever, but that's okay because their brand of rugby is a particularly virile and passionate one which always makes it interesting. Like all predominantly Latin peoples, the Argentinians are hardest to beat when they're playing on their own soil, but every 10km further they get away from Ground Zero home is another few points down on the Richter scale of the earthquake they are capable of creating. If the World Cup were to be held in Argentina itself, then the Argies might be a good chance to at least get to the semi-finals, but as it is, I fear they will merely serve as prime fodder for the bigger teams to chew on.

Australia

It's a tough one. As I see it, virtually the whole success or otherwise of Australia's World Cup campaign depended on whether or not they picked me. If they did, it would have displayed an intelligence, a vision, a wisdom that would be illustrative of our leaders' superb command of the situation and there could be no doubt that our national fortune was in good hands. The World Cup would be practically ours, I tell you.

But with me or without me, our style will remain much the same: physical, robust, have-a-go-yer-mug. Not for us the finely calibrated play of the Japanese, nor the cautious Geoffrey Boycott-like play of the English. We are somewhat, for mine, a cross between the bash 'ems of New Zealand and the 'run-it' attitude of the French.

Perhaps our greatest strength is that, more than most other nations, we Australians like running into other people—a crucial prerequisite for success in rugby. Don't you remember when you were a kid at primary school all those games you'd play which would somehow involve knocking other people over or being knocked over yourself? Well I do, and I've seen our kids happily knock each other over all over Australia, but I've never seen the same enthusiasm for it anywhere else—not in England, France, Italy or anywhere.

Whether it's something they put in our water supply I know not, but it's there and it has allowed Australia to compete and succeed at an international level, when numerically, in terms of players to pick from, we should be one of the easybeats of world rugby.

As to how the nation stands at the moment, the short answer is: not too shabby. We have the world's best half-back in Nick Farr-Jones, the world's leading Test try-scorer in winger David Campese and the world's leading Test points-scorer in five-eighth Michael Lynagh. They are the hub, heart and soul of the team and have been for damn nigh the past decade. Their experience should count for a lot when the business end of the tournament comes around, and there is quite an embarrassment of riches in other positions as well.

So who is going to win the mongrel? I'm stuffed if I know. But most of the smart money seems to be going down on New Zealand, Australia and England. New Zealand because they have the All Blacks, who in the absence of the Springboks are the most successful international team by the proverbial country mile. Australia, because they are the only team to have beaten the All Blacks in the past few yonks and it is generally considered that in the cyclical phases all football teams go through, its position on the bicycle wheel is somewhere right up there near the top. And England, because much of the World Cup will be played on their home turf, and there are some signs that after years of ultra-shabby performances they are starting to finally awaken and wrest their rightful place on the rugby totem pole.

There is another body of opinion which suggests that France, which made it to the final of the last World Cup, might be in a dangerous enough mood to repeat the performance and go one better, but for mine, while they are capable of beating anyone in the world on their day, those days usually fall only when they are in France, and neither the final nor the semi-finals are to be played there, so I figure they'll be up against it.

As to Scotland, you wouldn't say that any smart money is going down on them to win the Cup, but at least some moderate IQ money is being placed on them to win, albeit at long odds.

Finally, there is a posse of people with crystal balls who say that if there is a blue moon in the month of October, if pigs fly and the earth suddenly were to start spinning the other way, then Wales might also get up.

AUSSIES ARE LOADED WITH GOLDEN BULLETS

There we were, the boys and I, fighting out in the deep jungles of New Zealand when the news came through . . . I wasn't selected for the World Cup and they were. I was wounded, I'd taken a big mortar right in the guts and couldn't go on. I knew it, they knew it.

'Don't worry,' they said. 'We'll leave you here, propped up against a tree with a rifle, some supplies and ammo—plus one bullet just for you in case it gets too bad—and as soon as things sort themselves out we'll send back help.'

I'm still waiting. From the constant 'boom-booms' I hear from our guns up at the battlefront, I gather the battle is going well for us but I'll be damned if anybody has come back to get me . . .

Actually, *(soft music here please, maestro)* I miss the guys.

Like our full-back Marty Roebuck . . . Few representative players have worked so hard yet been beset by so many misfortunes as Marty. Over the years, if it wasn't his ankle, it was his knee, if not his knee, then a rare bad game at the wrong time. But somehow, against all odds Roebuck burst out and started dancing.

Then there's Bob Egerton, our flying winger. So often in rugby, as in life, someone's success is tied to someone else's failure. The really nice thing about Egerton's succession is that it came about precisely because of Roebuck's success. Egerton was originally called in as a late back-up full-back to Roebuck on the New South Wales tour to Argentina. Never played winger in his life. But with Roebuck playing so well, there was nowhere else for Bob to play than as a stop-gap winger and, joy of all joys, he made tries fall from the skies—and has done so ever since.

And David Campese . . . Not a lot more to say really. He's a good 'un and undoubtedly the best attacking player in the world.

The guys working inside Campo, shovelling out the really hot ammo at just the right time are of course, our centres Jason Little and Tim Horan. They're live ones, those two. One time in France, the whole squad had been ambushed and shot up pretty bad by some French dive-bombers and it really looked as if we were going to have to bite the big one, when these two guys suddenly took over the show and started shellacking the French from all angles.

Given confidence, the rest of us suddenly tore out of the trenches too, and gave the French a good pounding ourselves. We eventually won a great victory in what was ever afterwards known as the Battle of Strasbourg. The almost intuitive understanding that exists between them is no fluke as they have been playing side by side since they were eleven years old in the backblocks of Queensland.

The not-so-secret weapon of the squad is Michael Lynagh—'The One O'Clock Gun' as the Wallabies know him. When he fires, the whole team fires. His goal-kicks may have gone awry this tournament but The Gun is still firing accurately and long, destroying all before it. Watch out if he gets the goal-kicking back too.

Then there is Nicko, son of Chico, father of Jaco, master of all he surveys—Nick Farr-Jones. If the Martians came down and said 'We're going to play a rugby match against you next Saturday and if we beat you we're going to turn your planet to sushi' then Nick would be my choice as captain and half-back of the earth team.

Up in the foot-slogging infantry there are also a few useful performers. The ageless Simon Poidevin, for example. He was playing for Australia when Noah first threw away his gumboots, and will probably still be playing 100 moons from now. A good man to have covering your back in the hand-to-hand stuff.

And Willie Ofahengaue. We found him in a raid to New Zealand, converted him to our cause and have been following him into battle ever since. Unless I miss my guess, Willie is currently featuring large in the nightmares of Test players from New Zealand, Wales, Western Samoa and Ireland. As they toss and turn in restless sleep, the same terrifying vision must come back to them: they have the ball, they are advancing up-field, the sun is on their face, the wind is in their hair, all is right with the world then, again, it's him!

Willie O . . . coming at them, two-storeys high, fast as a runaway truck. Wham! They are awash in pain and the ball has floated away to who knows where. After the final, my guess is this recurring nightmare will also be showing up all over England.

Now, what really gets me, as I sit under this tree, is my old buddy and second-row partner Rod McCall. I mean, even as we speak, Rod is sleeping in my bed at the team hotel. Come on Rod, get up. The joke's over, you and Bob Dwyer have had your little laugh at my expense, making me think I was really going to miss out but don't you think you're taking it a bit far now? I mean, the final is tomorrow. I've got a field-phone with me, I've got the passport, and I'm ready to go.

As for his partner, John Eales, why, only a short time ago he was dubbed 'a player of the future'. Hear that John? Future, F-U-T-U-R-E. Not *now*. How dare you get your tenses mixed up? And I don't care if you are able to leap tall buildings at a single bound. Get off the bus and come back here and get me.

Look, I almost can't go on. But quickly, hooker Phil Kearns is our modern answer to the Sherman tank— undoubtedly the prototype for the rugby player of the year 2000. You'll be hearing a lot more from him for years to come. And the props . . . On a wet Monday some two years ago, the then all-but-anonymous Tony Daly underwent an Australian Rugby Union test to see how much he could benchpress. If I remember correctly, Daley benched some- thing like 170kg and in three days was on his way to New Zealand to make his Test debut at Eden Park. If you're reading this Bob Dwyer, I might just mention in passing that only yesterday I benched 200kg.

I'm almost as strong as Ewen McKenzie, the other prop. And if Ewen's not actually the strongest tight-head prop in the world he could probably fit into a phone booth with the guys ahead of him. He is also that rarest of the prop species who can not only spell 'cut-out pass!', he can also do one. Which leaves us with the coaches. The brutes.

Bob Dwyer stands a good chance of being hailed as the messiah of world rugby, in the same way that Alan Jones once was, if the Wallabies get up. He is ably supported by Bob Templeton the assistant coach. The grand old man of Australian rugby, Tempo is also a very capable coach but his role is more than that. If the Wallabies were to develop a dance around a sacred totem pole, Tempo's face would loom large at the very top of the pole. He is the deeply respected elder of the Wallaby tribe. And finally Jake Howard, the assistant assistant coach. His place on the totem pole is just below that of Tempo's.

So that's them. And that's me. Goodbye cruel world. Any calls for me? Where's that bullet . . .

MEMO TO THE WALLABIES

Oh yeah, sure. Like, we're meant to be impressed or something? You guys come back here, strutting around like superstars because you win some little tin-pot trophy called the World Cup which wouldn't even melt down into making a decent hub-cap? You want maybe we should get another fifteen stars on the national flag just for you?

I mean, just because you pulverise the All Blacks and beat our most cherished enemies, the English, in the final; just because you charm the world's press into thinking you're really a bunch of well-behaved, unpretentious, swell fellows who are a credit to the nation; just because, unlike many of the other teams, you were always available for interviews and chats with the locals and never acted like you were the ants' pants or the mossies' cossies . . . we're now meant to kowtow or something?

Perhaps you think a little bit of thundering applause might be in order? Like, you probably also think that just because you've now got a pretty good hold on a notable spot in international sporting history, because you bought great international glory to Australia, because all over the world there are a million rugby teams and you're the very best there is around on the planet at the moment, and not only that, you played in a fashion that would make a rugby man weep with pride—thrilling the soul of rugby and non-rugby lovers alike—because you've got 25 of the best 26 players in Australia in your ranks (ohallright26ofthe-best26) a little bit of light adulation mightn't go astray.

Maybe we should hold the ticker-tape parade down Wallaby Way and forget that boring old name of George Street? And you, Farr-Jones. So what if you're the best half-back in the world? You probably think it's kinda special that if we lost the moon to the Martians in a game of craps and had to play those morons double or nothing in a game of rugby to try to win it back, then you would be the man the United Nations would ask to be captain and half-back to knock those uppity Martians over? Really, so blooming *what*?

As for the rest of you, you're no doubt under the impression that a lot of us here in Australia were envious of you over there, that we really wished we could be playing with you. Well, that's where you were wrong. I mean, *dead wrong*. In fact, we had a helluva time back here, a real *helluva* time. Big party at Bob Hawke's place, all sixteen million of us getting to know each other for the first time. And only a paltry three million or so watching the footy in his living room when it came on. Gee, the party was great. Sorry you couldn't be there, really we were.

But noooooooooo, you had to go gallivanting off around the world, playing your way into history. Big deal. And today you're having a ticker-tape parade through the streets of Sydney. Like maybe you think you're the only football team ever accorded such an honour? Well, as a matter of fact you are, but maybe that's just because Nick Greiner thought of a clever way to get rid of all that tape that's been clogging up all those back rooms all these years.

All you did is create a bit of history, play great football, and ratchet the nation's self-esteem up a point or two in these trying times. Woop-de-bloody-doo. Don't go getting ideas like we're impressed or anything.

PSST! WANT TO KNOW THE SECRET FORMULA OF AUSTRALIA'S WORLD CUP WINNING TEAM?

Let us say, for argument's sake, that a country, any country, has serious ambitions to win the next World Cup. So serious that they engage a spy to look into the way that Australia did it. What would he come up with?

Ahem, well, he might say: 'Look around for a coach with the same make-up as Alan Jones, Australia's coach from 1984 to 1987.' That is to say, the sort of person with enough energy to move single-handedly the Great Pyramid of Cheops ten paces to the right if its aspect was not quite to his satisfaction; someone who, if he might not know the last word about the game of rugby, at least would know how to extract the last ounce of energy from his charges, and how to make them win.

Then, this guy would have to take the game of rugby and break it down into all its individual parts, from tackling to passing, from rucking to jumping, and all those in between. He would ensure that each player relentlessly polished all his skills until they gleamed.

Then, with the help of experts he would put it all back together again, and ruthlessly tune it, change it, tune it some more, change it, throw out old parts, bring in new, until it became so good that his team's very presence on a field would be enough to make the grass wilt and the goalposts come to their knees in submission. For two or three years, his reign of terror as coach should continue, constantly bullying his team into brilliant performances and mercilessly working them, until his charges, as good as they are, cry out: 'That's enough; there's nothing left!'

A brief mutiny, and then you must bring in the next coach, one who would take a different tack.

This guy should have big, owlish glasses, a little like Bob Dwyer's and he should also have a lot of fresh ideas though still building on the work of the first. He should be absolutely crackerjack with all the latest in sports science, and for a little light reading before bed, he should like to frolic naked through Kinsey's *Muscle Fibres, Mucus and Myaptic Membranes: How They Apply to Rugby*. And when the players whinge about having to go through all that nonsense, he should persist regardless. In the same way as the first coach, those players who cannot adapt to the changing times must be left by the wayside. But an essential part of the building process must be always to look out for new talent to work into the side. There should be a long queue of eligible champions waiting to get on board for those dropped off.

And if a country is really keen to win the World Cup, then a system should be instituted whereby young talent is spotted early and technical assistance offered them in the way of specialised coaching, dietary information, muscle-stretching, psychological preparation, ad bleeding nauseam.

But to go with all this, the second coach should also have tremendously innovative ideas about the game which are so complex it is only after a few years of his instruction that even his own players, let alone the opposition, get the hang of it. One other thing. Somewhere around and between these two succeeding coaches with their different styles, should be another fellow, an older one who helps out with the coaching and is universally loved by every member of the team. If you liken your national team to a tribe, then this guy must be the most revered tribal leader, someone a little like the Australian assistant coach, Bob Templeton.

This tribal elder must, around the fireside and the dinner table, constantly regale the team with stories of Test teams past to imbue them with a sense of history and destiny. Amid all the scientific and new-fangled mumbo-jumbo that is going on, it will be precisely the survival of this sense of history, and feeling of answerability to the glory of past teams, which will prove invaluable. (It may sound weird in the sober light of day, but such things really do work around the fire, and most importantly in the last ten minutes of tight matches.)

There, that is pretty much a blueprint of how to win in the next World Cup.

5 THE PLAYERS

RUGBY'S BRAVE SURVIVORS ARE WINNING ANOTHER WAR

At the time of his accident Peter Haylen was a student with two years to go to complete his degree in mechanical engineering. Although it took a year in hospital and another in rehabilitation before he could resume his studies, Haylen graduated recently and is seeking employment.

He would like a job where he can capitalise on his degree and 'make so much money I could really let fly'. Letting fly includes 'travelling, becoming more independent . . . and more travelling'. Haylen's chances of being employed will improve in little more than a month when he regains his driver's licence—this time in a specially equipped car.

He has gradually regained the use of his arms and hands, although not as yet his fingers, and says that 'some feeling' has returned to his legs. Part of the proceeds from the trust fund set up in his name by Sydney University Rugby Club has been used to remodel his home in suburban Northbridge to accommodate the use of his wheelchair.

Although acknowledging that occasionally he feels bitter about his misfortune, he says, 'I try not to think about the accident at all. When I do feel bitter I usually do some activity that takes my mind off it, like painting.' While a single painting can take him between two and three months his enthusiasm remains and he believes 'I become more adept with each effort'. The painting that takes pride of place in his bedroom is one of his father, who died at the end of last year.

His mother usually helps him with the things he cannot do independently. He refers to her as 'my personal saint' but hopes, in time, he will rely on her less and less. He was watching the match on television three years ago when Grant Harper was flown from the ground after being injured playing against Sydney University.

When a collapsing scrum in a club rugby match in 1984

91

left Western Suburbs player Grant Harper a quadriplegic he thought his life had also collapsed. For a start he believed that his career at the Department of Sport and Recreation was over. He was wrong.

Four years later he is again part of the department's workforce but the legacies of a severe spinal injury in the game against Sydney University remain severe. Below the neck, his only functioning muscle is the left bicep. But a combination of modern technology, government support and old-fashioned grit has allowed him to assume a new role with the department as a data-base programmer for the NSW Sports Council for Disabled People.

Working out of an office in the State Sports Centre at Homebush, he is able to operate the computer keyboard and the telephone with his mouth-stick, and the limited movement in his left arm permits him to manoeuvre his motorised wheelchair around the office. The other essential piece of equipment is his desk.

The desk, designed and built by his late grandfather, has been raised to the optimal height, has accommodating slits cut into it for the wheelchair arms and slats of wood nailed into the top which keep the keyboard in a set position.

Harper is no longer as quick and efficient as he was, but it is a lesson in the dimensions of human adaptation to see the speed and dexterity with which he now uses his mouth-stick. Although a single metal rod will never be as effective as ten fingers in flicking over the keys, he is still closing the gap. As for the effect that working again has had on his life, he is just south of 'ecstatic'.

'I was sick to death of staying home all the time,' he said. 'And I was going crazy with boredom. Though I managed to keep busy it was more just time-filling stuff that didn't have any real depth to it. Now I'm actually contributing something and it feels great.'

Harper said the social aspects of his job were also important. 'The injury I suffered was bad and the pain was bad but one of the worst things for people like me is suddenly being cut off from the rest of the world and becoming so totally isolated. Now that I'm working again

I'm back into the social mainstream and moving again. Just being able to meet people and relate to them on a level other than normal person/quad is a joy to me.'

Another benefit of Harper's return to work is that his wife, Cathy, no longer has to look after him all day. She has resumed her job as a special education teacher's aide. An organisation known as Home Care arranges visits to Harper's office three times a day to provide the care that all quadriplegics need regularly.

As for Harper's future, he believes that although he is 'very content with the present situation' he doesn't feel that he has yet found his niche and hopes eventually to move on to other work.

'I am not really sure what I want to get into, but I feel that there are other avenues I would like to explore which might be more beneficial to the department and more fulfilling for me personally,' he said. This is possible, according to the department's deputy director, John Stathers, one of the men most responsible for Harper's re-employment. 'We are very happy with Grant's work so far and in that particular position he's performing as well as someone without disabilities,' Stathers said. 'There has been no special treatment accorded to Grant and I know he doesn't want any. In looking to the future I would say this: Grant is becoming increasingly adept with computers and that is where the future lies . . . Whatever problems there are with his body there's obviously nothing wrong with his brain, and that is all that counts in this kind of work.'

It also counts to have a supportive and understanding employer.

ONCE MORE WITH FEELING; A WINGER'S PRAYER

It is an odd sort of happy story. The misery gauge only shifted from 'total tragedy' to 'grave misfortune', but everyone seems delighted all the same.

With four minutes to go in the first half of the NSW v Waikato game at Concord on Saturday, Waratah winger Chris Saunders received the ball, swivelled, and at the precise moment he passed the ball, was hit from behind in a legal tackle.

And he could still hear them, all the yelling of the players and the yahooing of the crowd as the game went on around him—but he was powerless to move. He lay numbly, lying on the ground with his face to the skies. He tried to move his legs—tried, tried and tried again but still they wouldn't move.

Then, as the game continued to move back and forth and the players had moved on from over the top of him, he was able to wave his right arm. He weakly tried to make himself heard: 'Stop the game, stop the game.'

The game moved on, oblivious, and he was still left there, trying to turn his head to an angle where he could see his legs. But that, too, was useless and he began to think 'about the paraplegic bloke next door, and how I might be . . .'

The obvious.

The way Saunders tells it, though, he was not hit with the sort of blind panic you might expect. Almost as if the numbness of his neck and legs had spread to his emotions, he was noting what was going on without feeling that he was a part of it all.

Now Waratah physiotherapist Ian Collier was bending over him. Now the other players were gathering around. Now team doctor Miles Coolican was pinching his legs and asking him questions. Now they were waving to the stands for someone to bring a stretcher.

It all seemed a little unreal.

Up in the stands his mother, Anne Taylor, was in no such state of suspended reality. From the first moment her son had gone down her eyes had stayed on him, and while the rest of the crowd followed the ball, she *willed* him to get up and dust himself off. But still he wouldn't move.

'I was thinking wheelchairs,' she said. 'I was sure he would be spending the rest of his life in a wheelchair, and had to restrain myself from running out on to the field immediately.'

She arrived at the players' exit tunnel with her husband and other son just the barest moment after the winger was carried from the field, and followed the crowd up to the NSW dressing-room door where, bizarrely, they were stopped by a security guard.

Inside the dressing-room, the first glimmer of hope came for Saunders as they took the strapping from his ankle and he could faintly feel the adhesive pulling a few hairs out.

'Not a lot, but I could feel it just enough to know that it wasn't totally dead down there,' he recalled.

Bit by bit over the next few minutes a little feeling started to come back to his feet, though still no movement. Saunders could hear the doctors for the first time start to make positive noises amid all the worry—things like 'spinal cord may be only bruised' and 'air ambulance not necessary'.

Over in the Spinal Care Unit at Royal North Shore Hospital that evening, at about 6.10 pm, he moved one foot for the first time, then moved it again, and it was almost like his parents wanted to break out champagne, such was the palpable relief.

By yesterday, Saunders had been discharged from the hospital to rest at home for the next two weeks.

Although he will have to wear a neck brace for a while and still has a strong feeling of pins and needles, it is expected he will regain full movement in all his limbs. He is, however, under strict medical instructions never to play rugby again—in fact, never even play so much as touch football—for fear of damaging what will forever be a weak point in his spinal column, but appears relatively untroubled by it.

This is in part because he remembers a small incident that happened in the early hours of Sunday morning in the hospital. Saunders was awake in his room, next to a fellow in the other bed, an 'incomplete' quadriplegic who had been in a bad surfing accident about 13 weeks ago.

'He had a respirator and had great difficulty speaking,' Saunders recalled. 'But he saw I was awake and asked how I was. I said, "Look, I can move my foot," and he looked and said very softly, so I could just hear him, "Lucky bastard".'

'That's pretty much what I think I am.'

An odd sort of happy story.

LE PETIT NAPOLEON AND THE YOUNG MAN FROM MOROCCO

The French Rugby Union touring party arrive here today for their three-Test tour. By the by, here are a couple of things about the most senior and junior members of the touring party, drawn from the four years I spent playing club rugby in France.

Jacques Fouroux

Le petit Napoleon is rather an apt nickname for this charismatically autocratic coach. On the two occasions that Fouroux coached me as part of the French Barbarians outfit, his style of coaching always reminded me of former American president Theodore Roosevelt's classic power maxim: 'Speak softly, and carry a big stick.'

In a sense, Fouroux is 'one of the boys' in his relationship with the team, never handing out his edicts as though he has just read them on a tablet sent from God . . . but nobody calls him 'baldy' all the same, despite his thinning hair.

In my book, his ability to mould a team is undoubted. In fifteen minutes flat, this ex-Test half-back had our French Barbarian scrum functioning well enough to trouble Ireland the following day, if not totally destroy them. He didn't do it by going into all the whys and wherefores of 'wrist positions', 'feet back' and 'dips in our back' etc. as is our Anglo-Saxon wont.

Rather, he harnessed his strong personality into the service of that curious French method of scrum coaching, which is to endlessly repeat phrases to the order of *C'est dans la tranche, les gars!* (it's all in the head, boys!), *Il faut avoir la coeur!* (you've got to do it with heart!) and occasionally beating his chest until we got *le feeling* . . . and got it right.

A few more minutes of that, with Jacques occasionally popping in and out of the scrum in various positions to show us how he wanted *le feeling* to manifest itself in physical action, and then we moved on to something far more interesting—like a game of touch.

So what do you do? You have the wind in your hair, the ball in your hands, Jacques Fouroux going like the clappers on your left and loudly purring for the ball, and Serge Blanco on the outside, obviously in the clear if only you do a cut-out pass on the French coach.

Of course, I gave it to Fouroux—it was the only decision possible. There's something about the guy that makes it impossible to execute a cut-out pass with him as the bunny. I should not be surprised if Daniel Dubroca, who is nominally the coach-elect of this French side, with Fouroux as part-coach part-manager, feels the same way.

Whatever their respective titles, Fouroux is the sort of person who is always going to be centre stage of any outfit he is a part of, and it would be very brave of Dubroca to give any cut-out directives to the team that Fouroux wasn't in full accordance with.

Abdelatif Bennazi

A couple of seasons ago, my club of Brive had a bye on the Sunday. To pass the time, a couple of us went to see a lowly second-division game of rugby between the nearby small towns of Souillac and Cahors.

It would have been an entirely Mickey Mouse affair except for one thing. In the middle of this rugby rabble stood one outstanding player—a young second-rower from Cahors who I'd never seen or heard of before. I really don't want to lay this on too thick, but as we watched in growing wonder this guy all but single-handedly destroyed the Souillac team with an athleticism, aggression and technique that is as rare as Moroccan rugby players in France.

Funnily enough, that's what he was. A Moroccan, by the name of Bennazi, who'd played rugby at school in Morocco, then lobbed at a cousin's house in Cahors, joined the club and gone on from there.

At the time of witnessing this revelation, I was ranked the No. 1 second-rower in France, (even if I do say so myself), and while I might have strutted into the stadium, an awful lot of swagger had gone out of my step by the time I slunk out, feeling quite wretched as I recall.

In short, I knew I'd be hearing more from him, however anonymous he was in his present circumstances. Not surprisingly, only two seasons on, here he is again, out here making his debut with the French team—one of the two foreigners in the touring party, the other being Eric Melville, the South African-born lock from Toulon. Still only 21, Bennazi is far and away the youngest of the touring party but my guess is he's also one of the most talented.

NEW LADS JOIN THE AUSSIE CAST

Marty Roebuck and Bob Egerton have just earned their first selection to the Australian Rugby Union Test team.

In this year of the World Cup, when every football player who can pull on a boot has made himself available, neither was expected to achieve such high honour. But they're there, against all odds.

Looking back, each will no doubt pinpoint the moment when he finally broke free from the thick pack of contenders for the throne. Perhaps the moments were these two . . .

Marty Roebuck

On the way back from Argentina, the New South Wales team stopped in New Zealand to play the North Harbour side. There was great interest in the game, not least because the 'Bring Back Buck' (Shelford) campaign was gaining momentum and Shelford was captaining North Harbour that day. Sure enough, twenty minutes into the second half Shelford, arguably the most damaging man with the ball in his hands in world rugby, gouged the ball from a maul and set off up-field . . . Three shoulder charges and one palm-off later, he was through. Almost. The only thing that remained between Shelford and the try line was the slender Roebuck.

Wha . . . wha . . . WHAM! In three precise movements, Roebuck drove his shoulder deep into Shelford's midriff, straightened his legs to lift him high above the field and then drove him straight into the turf. The mud splattered at Shelford's point of impact.

Around the ground, the momentary stunned silence gave way to an excited buzzing. On the field, Marty gazed down upon his still prone and dazed quarry with the truly appalled expression of one who didn't even know his gun was *loaded*, let alone pointing in such a dangerous direction . . . but by then it was too late. The damage was done.

The Bring Back Buck campaign was derailed and Marty—*toot, toot!*—was slowly shunting his engine the other way with a Roebuck For Test Full-back banner on it. His engine gained momentum as the season progressed.

Bob Egerton

Every good winger has his own ace of spades to play when the occasion warrants. Ian Williams has pure, blinding speed. David Campese has his amazing step. Bob Egerton has, somehow, the ability to know instinctively where the gap will appear before it is actually there. In club rugby, at full-back, he has long been noted for zigging when the defence thought he would zag . . . and zagging when the defence thought he would zig. But previous to this season he has never had the opportunity to show his wares at the representative level, and never before on the wing at any level.

Bob's real moment of awakening in the selectors' consciousness surely came in the NSW–Queensland game, at Ballymore. With only minutes to go, Queensland were ahead and the first strains of a fat lady singing were just starting to fill the stands. Suddenly though, from broken play, New South Wales outside centre Craig Wells cut through the defence on the left flank and charged down the field with Egerton haring along just outside him.

The Queensland tacklers all focused on the obvious danger and primed themselves to put both Egerton and Wells into touch. But at the precise moment when they were committed to that option, Egerton cut back inside Wells and proceeded to the goal-line on a clear super-highway that the Queenslanders hadn't even seen, let alone bothered to put roadblocks upon.

When Egerton put the ball down between the posts for the winning try he had just set his own Test-wagon a'rolling.

Whether these players go on with it to stack up another twenty caps or so, is anybody's guess. They've both kept very good players out of the team, players who will be essaying to reclaim their spots as the season progresses. That's the game.

But even those players left out will probably take some pleasure, in spite of themselves, that two guys who for so long have been in the wings of Australian rugby, so long threatening to happen without ever quite getting there, have finally got on to centre-stage just at a time when it seemed likely that the curtain had drawn for them. Good on them both.

WILLIE O.—A GLIMPSE OF A DIFFERENT SORT OF MAN

Willie O. really didn't want to stay for the after-match function and neither did I. So a quick 'LOOK!' to the left, as we ducked to the right, then through a door, out a window, down a fire escape, and we were out into the drizzly Wellington night. And not a taxi to bless ourselves with.

There was nothing for it but to walk back to the hotel, half an hour away. Trudging, trudging, trudging along. So, who is this man beside me, anyway? What does anybody know about Willie Ofahengaue, other than that he's from Tonga, plays a football game straight out of hell, and is a very good and likable man? Willie doesn't give interviews and is excruciatingly embarrassed by his own fame.

If given a choice, he would walk four blocks out of his way to avoid a single question from a journalist. But this time I had him. We had to walk 30 blocks together, and as I was cleverly disguised as a fellow footballer, there was nothing for him to do but to answer a few questions.

Did he enjoy the World Cup?

'Yes.'

Did he love playing for the Wallabies?

'Yes.'

Did he want to go to Rugby League?

'No.'

Did he come across any racism when he was recently in South Africa?

'No.'

Trudging, trudging, trudging along. No, it wasn't the stuff from which Pulitzer Prizes are made, but it was a start . . . and besides, that was at least four Willie quotes that, with his permission, I could put in a story—which was a lot more than most Willie profiles could claim.

Trudging, trudging. Sometimes, surely, people must mistake Willie's reticence to speak for a lack of the smarts. It is not. As a small example, there are more than ten

103

possible moves that can be made from the back of the scrum in the New South Wales team. The rest of us have been trying to get them securely in our heads for the past four months.

Only one player has never joined our discussion of them. Willie had them from the first moment he heard them. Never asked a question, never made a mistake.

Although these preplanned moves go against the grain of the way he would prefer to operate—admitting once, in a rare moment of verbosity that he would prefer to 'just play'—it is enough that this is what the coach wants. No arguments from Willie.

And the rest of us, in the minute before going on to the field, do all manner of things to get ourselves into a suitably aggressive frame of mind. We jump, sit, wave our arms, punch our palms—anything. Willie prays. Not ostentatiously, so as you'd even notice—and it is not clear whether he prays for himself or the safety of his opposition—but that is what he does. And the rest of us sometimes get drunk, sometimes have smoked. Willie has done none of these things—ever. His strong Christianity forbids it, and for him that is the end of the section.

Yet he never has even the slightest 'forbidding' air about him in the middle of our worst excesses. Let it be, each to his own.

And how is it that Willie can be the most feared forward in the international game—featuring large in the nightmares of players from Auckland to Tokyo to London—yet has never raised an unprovoked fist in anger, or even engaged in mildly untoward rucking? A different sort of man to be sure.

The hotel is up ahead. Whaddya say we go to the bar and get smashed, Willie?

'No, Fitzy.'

A small smile and a shake of the head. Suddenly, in the back window of a parked van in front of the hotel pops up a little boy's smiling face. Then another, then another. Uncle Willie is back. Out of the small van comes an impossibly-large number of people, Tongans all.

In the middle of the throng, Willie turns and says: 'Family. See ya.'

See ya Willie.

A different sort of man.

TIM GAVIN—A RARE COMBINATION

It was in Christchurch just before the First Test against the All Blacks in 1990. Bobby Nasser, the then Wallaby back-rower, was in his usual ruminative mood and had just had some sort of particularly heavyweight inspiration.

'You know,' he said, turning to me as that vague look he often has on his face lightened for a moment, 'Tim Gavin is just the sort of bloke you'd choose to have beside you if you had to charge up over the top of the trenches and into the teeth of the enemy.'

True enough. Tim Gavin is *exactly* that sort of bloke, and many is the rugby player who has been glad to have Tim beside him in a particularly tight spot.

Which is not the only reason so many Wallabies have expressed thanksgiving that, after missing out on the World Cup through injury, Gavin is now back in the side playing in his favoured No. 8 position against Scotland last week in the First Test and again tomorrow.

It's also because Gavin is now undisputed as the best in the business of No. 8 in the world. Ball-winning ability is not new in a No. 8, nor is heart, nor power, nor creativity, nor extraordinary toughness. But the combination of all five in just the one player is new enough, and rare enough, that Gavin is rightly celebrated because of it.

The odd thing is that Gavin should have achieved such pre-eminence without most of the public having any clear idea as to what sort of a man he is. Somehow, the profiles and so forth that have attached themselves to other players have not fastened upon him.

Let it then be said: Gavin is, as Australians go, a particularly *Australian* sort of Australian. Son of the soil, that sort of thing. Born and raised on a farm in Cumnock in western New South Wales, as part of a large family, he came to school in Sydney in the mid-1970s and learnt his rugby there. Adulthood saw him playing with the Easts club, taking whatever jobs he could find through the winter so as to pursue his rugby, and then in the summer he either headed home to the farm, or north to Queensland, where he would spend months driving cattle trucks in Goondiwindi. The spirit of Banjo Paterson was surely lurking somewhere around.

Last year, just when his form was right at its peak, when the Wallabies were only weeks away from their most historic foreign expedition, he suffered a knee injury in a simple club match that would put paid to all thoughts of playing rugby for a good six months.

Looking back on it now he is relatively sanguine, though at the time it was enough to make his custard curdle.

'It wasn't just that I was going to miss out on the World Cup,' he said. 'It was that I was forced to leave a really tightly-knit team that was playing fantastic rugby, after we had all been through so much together to get to that point.

'It was like being forced off the train at Wyong, and leaving all my mates, when I'd paid my ticket all the way to Central.'

The truth of the matter is that without him, many of the Wallabies weren't sure that the train would get to Central at all, though happily their fears proved unfounded.

Gavin's plans for the future extend at least to the end of next year before he 'takes another look at it'.

'After that,' he says, 'it depends on how things are going on the land. If things are good enough to support my return, then maybe I'll go home and if not, then maybe I'll give it another year.'

The moral of the whole story? None particularly. Just heartening to see a good man taking back his spot in a good team. A worthy heir to the legacy of Mark Loane and Steve Tuynman, Gavin overcame the latter, and receives regular phone calls of support and advice from the former.

6 THE GAME

IT'S NOT THAT HARD ONCE YOU GET THE HANG OF IT

If you had to explain to an awoken Rip Van Winkle about major modern sports, how long would it take? Soccer. About 30 seconds: one ball, two teams, two goals, put ball through goal, fall about on ground all over each other. The only complexities that he would have to grasp are the offside rule and the fact that when any player gets even the mildest tap on the ankle he has to writhe about on the ground for a good minute or so until the penalty is milked.

Golf. Another 30 seconds: one ball, several clubs, eighteen holes, much cursing, long walks. Tenpin bowling. Three seconds. The name of the game says it all. Darts. Ditto. Tennis. Five to ten minutes.

Rugby Union. Listen Rip, sit down here and make yourself comfortable, this is going to take a while. And don't start to nod off. For the uninitiated, rugby is not an easy game to comprehend and its very complexity is enough to ensure that it will never get the 60–70 per cent following that soccer is able to garner in many countries.

Despite reports, it's not just any moron who is able to play or watch rugby. It takes a special type. To the novice, a game of rugby looks like an impossible tangle of arms and legs that occasionally dissembles, forms up into humans, charges across the field to then become another impossible tangle. It is only by knowing about the rules of the game that it all starts to make sense, but therein lies another problem.

Unlike most other sports, what the rules say should happen in rugby, and what actually happens, are only second cousins once removed. Take for example the line-out. This, like many parts of the rugby game, is simple in theory, chaotic in practice and according to the strict letter of the sporting law, all line-outs are illegal.

Well and verily might it say in the official and most blessed rugby rule book that: '. . . and God said unto Moses, from this point forth there will be a metre of space

111

between the shoulders of team-mates in the rugby line-out and a half-metre corridor between them and their opponents and yea, so too will there be no movement across this corridor until the ball has landed on the furthest fingertips of one of the players.'

There hasn't been a line-out like this ever and certainly not in the 1991 World Cup. Someone with one eye on the TV and one eye on the rule book would no doubt still have no idea of what is going on. In fact, the real name of the game is for both teams to charge across the narrow corridor separating them as soon as the ball has left the hands of the thrower.

They do this with much the same alacrity with which the Germans charged across the Rhineland all those years ago, and for much the same reasons. It is done both to bustle the opposition and to enlarge your territory so as to maximise the chances that when the ball spills downwards, it will fall to you and not the opposition.

Savvy Rippa? It's like this all through the rugby game. It may actually say in the rule book that '. . . and Yea, when a penalty is awarded, all infidels and heathens and opposing teams will move back across the River of Jordan, a distance of precisely ten metres'.

In fact, the convention is that this does not mean 'that distance between nine and eleven metres'. It means 'back a bit' (usually about five metres). When it says in the rule book that 'a player will release the ball as soon as his body is on the deck', it means 'only if he stands a good chance of being seen by the referee'.

Do you get it, Rip? It's a game that is such a natural expression of the basic urge that some people feel to run into each other, that the rules don't actually fit precisely over the game itself, and never have been able to. You need a referee who understands that and will let the booger go.

And the really curious thing about it is that, more than any other game, Test teams tend to play in a fashion evocative of their national spirit. In the World Cup we saw the flair and derring-do of the French, the dour grittiness of the New Zealanders, the technically excellent precision of the Japanese, the overwhelming exuberance of the Western Samoans and the solid, stolid, stuffy and downright boring play of the English.

And how did our guys play? In the spirit of the nation from which they sprang. If you could take one of our most famous sporting phrases: 'Have a go yer mug', and turn it into a style of playing football, then that has been the Wallaby way. What's that Rip? You think you've got the drift and you'd like to go have a good lie-down? Okay, but make sure you set the alarm for the 1995 World Cup final.

WHEN PUSH CAME TO SHOVE IT WAS GREAT

I compose these words on my mental typewriter while I heave away in the middle of the mud heap that is currently Sydney University's No. 2 oval. Little matter that the bottom part of my football boots has disappeared into terra liquida, that the rain is roaring down, that the wind is screaming imprecations at the devil, that the world beyond this oval has seemingly shut down. My colleagues and I are here on very, very serious business and *goddammit*, we intend to do it, cyclone or no cyclone.

Once again . . . *ka-thud* . . . we smash into each other, eight tightly bound men against eight others, and once again . . . *ker-splat* . . . the whole thing collapses and my dial goes right into the fetid slush.

This is scrum training. As you may or may not know, the scrum is that part of the Rugby Union game which involves sixteen fully grown men pushing on either side of a ball to decide who gets possession of it next.

Personally, I'd be in favour of tossing a coin, or perhaps having the referee hold his whistle in one hand while the two captains tried to guess which one he had it in . . . but that's another story.

Back in the here and now, we're trying to overcome a problem. Our scrum last Saturday was nothing short of disgraceful and this little session is designed to work out what went wrong. Fortunately, at least a good part of it is talk. Sydney Uni's resident scrum guru, Tony Abbot, is in full flight. Through the howling gale, I can just make out his words . . . Turn . . . your . . . wrists . . . tighterrrr . . .

We hit it again, all turning our wrists tighter (to bind us more closely together) and accentuating the dip in our backs (if I could understand why this was so important I could be the guru).

Sure enough, the pressure on us in this scrum is marginally more unbearable than the last one, so we know we

114

must be doing something right. The *ker-splat* seems to be taking a little longer this time and I ponder, while my face is rhythmically rubbed between the muddy thighs of the prop and the hooker (the two men in front of me), whether I just might get out of this scrum without having to wallow like a little piggy.

But no, the *ker-splat* makes its appearance soon enough, and we all get down in the mud for a good roll round. Even before we have picked ourselves up, Abbot is off and running, as is his wont, through the sheets of rain to a new scrum position down-field.

It is his theory that a good scrum-training session must obligatorily be interspersed with these short sprints so it is as near to a game situation as possible. Ours is not to reason why—so we reluctantly stumble on after him. By now looking like a pack of mutant muddy wombats, we prepare to pack down a new scrum. But first we must do the ritual shouting.

'Seconds ball!' yells Abbot (it is the turn of seconds to introduce the ball to the scrum). 'Low!' yells the hooker (we must make sure our body position is very low for maximum force). '102!' yells the prop (this is a TOP SECRET code number which indicates to the pack what sort of push we are going to use to try to recover the ball).

All the proprieties observed, we pack the scrum down . . . and try to remember all the many things we are meant to be doing with all the different parts of our body to maximise the force on the opposing pack. Suddenly . . . a . . . *miracle*. Be darned if it is not working. Joy of all joys, pleasure of all pleasures! Somehow, magically, we have gone from being a disparate group of eight individuals, pushing disjointedly, into being fused as one.

Centimetre by muddy centimetre, we can feel the opposing pack giving ground as in unison, in harmony, we inexorably turn the screws tighter. The rain has stopped, the wind has fallen, we are as one. The muddy field is but a pristine stage on which we can perform our artistry. Is it our imagination or can we hear the strains of Brahms Fifth Symphony wafting over us as we push?

Ker-splat! It is over. We wake up in the mud again. Sad, but immeasurably richer for the experience. Nirvana has been reached, for however fleeting a moment.

PLOTTING A NEW FRENCH REVOLUTION

Paris, Monday: If the French forward pack of years gone by were turned by some method into points of punctuation, the composition of the pack would look something like the following. The two props would be full stops (..) anchoring the scrum.

The hooker would be a question mark (?) designed specifically for hooking the ball back. The second-rowers would be a couple of tall timber slashes (/ /) trying to keep low, and the back-rowers would be all exclamation marks (!!!) ready to explode into action at a moment's notice.

Thus, from numbers one to eight the French line-up would be: .?.//!!! Contrast this with the line-up of the pack coach Jacques Fouroux is planning to put on the field for France in the World Cup of 1991: !!!!!!!! Get it? In Fouroux's conception of la rugby moderne, *everyone* must be mobile, explosive and dynamic and there is no longer a place for forwards that specialise in only a single facet of the game.

To aid and abet his dream of having only exclamation marks in his team, Fouroux has this year completely revolutionised the French scrum. He has done so by embracing a formerly obscure Argentinian scrum concept called *La Bajadita*. This is designed to overcome, among other things, the need for human full stops playing at prop. Its essence lies in the way the forwards bind with each other.

First, the two props reverse their usual stances. The loose-head prop has his right foot forward and his left foot back while the tight-head prop has his left foot forward and his right foot back.

The second-rowers no longer bind between the thighs of their props but rather around their waists and the hooker now binds his arms under the arms of his props. Believe it or not, the hooker does not now hook, dedicating himself entirely to pushing. So it is no longer necessary to select a traditional hooker and in fact in the French opener

117

against Ireland in Dublin in 1988, the French No. 2 was 30-year-old Phillipe Morocco who had previously only ever played prop.

Ideally, the ball comes back to the French pack either because they are going forward or because the ball hits the foot of one of the props and is then deflected backwards.

The most interesting thing about it is that it works. In the four Test matches that the French have played so far this season, they have used *La Bajadita* to great effect, and in the Test against Romania the French even went so far as to demonstrate their mastery of the new method by having half-back Henri Sanz introduce the ball from the tight-head side.

They won the ball all the same. Why doesn't the opposing hooker hook? Because all of the scrum's force is arrowed directly into him and the only way for him to withstand this enormous pressure is to push in return, with both feet back.

To quote *Midi Olympique*, France's rugby bible, *La Bajadita* is 'a revolution which, while requiring less pure strength for the team using it, can aid in exhausting opposing players that may be more dynamic, and in such fashion help our side develop the continuity of their play'.

The goal therefore, is not to leave all one's energy in the scrum but to conserve it for where it really counts, in the open play. Revolutionising the scrum in such a way has not been done in isolation but is part of Fouroux's wider conviction that the road to glory for French rugby lies with a far more dynamic physical type of play for forwards and backs alike.

Fouroux explains: 'This year, the forwards must learn to move around the field in the same direction. They must know that when they lift their head from the scrum they have a rendezvous at such or such a place and be capable of transforming themselves instantaneously into backs if the situation warrants.

'In return, the backs must be capable, after a breakthrough from one of their own, to transform themselves into forwards and form a beachhead on the tackled player

118

. . . upon which the real forwards can launch themselves when they arrive.'

In short, if Fouroux's plans come to fruition France will eventually field fifteen exclamation marks and not just the habitual three. Of course, enthusiasm for Fouroux's revolutionary ideas has not been universal and in response to his plans for ! ! ! there has been a lot of flak coming from the purists who maintain he's gone way beyond the bounds of his charter as national coach. Traditionally, revolutions are a process of 'breaking down rotten doors' and a good many French rugby people maintain that far from being rotten, the traditional methods of French play, *le French flair*, have worked well for decades.

So why change it now? In a regular Sunday night sports show for example, France's answer to Rex Mossop, Pierre Salviac, showed selected segments of the French play against Romania and characterised it as 'Rambomania'. His particular lament was that French rugby was moving too far from its natural roots. In the weeks that followed, oceans of ink were spilt in either lambasting or supporting Fouroux's new program and as I write, the debate here rages on in its inimitable Gallic fashion.

But whether Fouroux wins or loses the wider battle is academic—*La Bajadita* itself is already a proven winner. Now, is there at least one enterprising coach out there willing to give it a try on Australian shores?

AFTER THE BRAWL IS OVER

A funny thing happened at a rugby dinner the other night. I was sitting next to Wallaby winger David Campese and happened to notice his shiny new autobiography sitting there on the table. By pure chance, I opened it on the exact page where it was written that Peter FitzSimons had started a brawl which had sullied rugby's good name.

My heart raced, my forehead broke out into a cold sweat. Thank God. At last it was over. At last I had been found out. I knew I was a killer who had managed to get away with it out on the field all these years, but now at last I had been publicly outed.

Thank God. And thank you, David, for making international rugby safe once again for decent law-abiding citizens. Please stop me before I kill again.

The accusation Campese makes is, although unfair, at least a pointer to an interesting phenomenon. Just about all the biff has gone out of football in the past few years.

In the old days, almost the defining feature of a good game was that it had a good brawl. But these days brawling is quite a rarity. And when it does occur—as it did in the altercation Campese refers to, in the opening minutes of the First Test against the French in 1990—it attracts enormous attention.

So, where has all the biffo gone? It has been killed off by:

Television In days of yore, the usual way for a brawl to begin was when someone king-hit someone else, shoved an elbow in the face in a tackle, or something equally dastardly.

These days if you do that you're more than likely to see yourself in full living colour, from sixteen different angles, not only on the nightly news, but also in a judiciary meeting the following Monday night where you could be suspended for weeks, if not months. Not only has 'video killed the radio star' as the song goes, it has also killed a lot of biffo.

Image And the reason that the administrators, particularly in rugby League, come down so hard with their suspensions is that they are keen to present clean, wholesome, family entertainment on the screen and forestall parents persuading their sons not to play such a rough game.

When you spend $2 million getting a world famous superstar in Tina Turner to sing your praises, you don't want some oaf breaking somebody's head on television and destroying all the good work.

Professionalism In the ultra-refined tactics and strategies that dominate the modern game, there is simply no place, or almost no place, for brawling. When the top-line footballers spend all their time out on the field concerned with angles of attack, umbrella defences, cut-out passes to loop left and jive chip kicks designed to bamboozle the defence, Cro-Magnon things like brawling have no place. As a tactic, it's horse-and-buggy stuff.

Law Once upon a time, the law of the land stopped at the edge of the field, where the referee was the only sheriff in those parts. Now, as has been shown in recent legal cases, assault is assault is assault and it doesn't matter where it occurs.

The old P.G. Wodehouse line that football is a game where 'each side is allowed to put in a certain amount of assault and battery and do things to its fellow man which, if done elsewhere, would result in 14 days without the option, coupled with some strong remarks from the bench . . .' no longer applies.

The law no longer makes an exception for what happens on the football field. All of which no doubt leaves us with a far better game to both watch and play. Now, only very rarely will a brawl break out.

Still biffo persists, ever so occasionally. How does it happen, precisely? Well, the mechanics of it are something like this: you file out on to the Sydney Football Stadium field, wearing your national colours, with fourteen of your countrymen, in front of 45 000 or more countrymen, and you sing the national anthem arm-in-arm and you line up to receive the kick-off and the adrenalin is coursing through your veins so much you're almost weeping with it.

Then in the first line-out, you'll cop an elbow in the mouth from your opposite number but you'll live with it, and in the second line-out you'll cop another one and you'll say 'right, THAT'S ENOUGH!' and then you'll start swinging 'em yourself.

Simple as that. And all hell will break loose. And some time later, you'll read about it with a certain acid amusement in Campo's colouring-in book. And that's about it. No particular big deal.

If I can get just one Rexism in before I go, though, it is this: personally I thought it wasn't only a good brawl, I thought it was a GREAT brawl. I thought everybody had a good time, no one was hurt and I know for a fact it is remembered by all participants with great affection.

There, I've said it. Now, please feel free to 'tut-tut' till your nose bleeds. You, too, King Tut-Tut.

7 THE TERMINOLOGY

THE FRENCH STICK THE BOOT INTO ENGLISH SPORTSPEAK

Après un match, dans le clubhouse, le star rugbyman est tres cool avec les fans. Après un fabuleux comeback (un hat-trick des drop goals), son team gagne une ko victoire, aux adversaires en un photo-finish.

Welcome to the wonderful world of Franglais . . . or 'Frenglish', if you will. Those familiar words in the above French text are, together with many other words and expressions of equally Anglo-Saxon origin, in common usage in the French sporting world.

Or at least were until recently. The rub is, that despite appearances it seems that these innocuous little words and expressions may not be so innocent after all . . .

How's that? Elementaire, my dear Clousseau. It has now been revealed that these Anglicisms and, most particularly, Americanisms, are actually dastardly examples of the rising damp of Coca-Colanisation in the Gallic culture and language, and as such must be liquidated.

So say the bureaucrats anyway. France for the French, keep the language pure, eyes right and all hail xenophobia. Briefly, the French government's commission on sporting terminology has just released a report detailing 30 English terms it wants expunged from French usage, and twenty others it recommends should no longer be used.

The commission, composed of journalists, sports officials, educators, grammarians and linguists, has spent more than two years identifying and isolating these alien terms and has determined what their red-blooded French replacements should be.

Here are some examples with their replacements in parenthesis: clubhouse (*maison de club*), comeback (*retour*), goal (*but*), goalkeeper (*gardien de but*), hat-trick (*coup de chapeau*), indoor *(en salle)*, meeting *(réunion sportive)*, offside *(hors jeu)*, out of bounds *(dehors)*, photo finish *(photo d'arrivee)*, referee *(arbitre)*, score *(marque)*, shot or kick *(tir)*, team *(équipe)*, time-out *(arrêt de jeu)*, toss *(tirage au sort)* and training *(entrainment)*.

And on it goes. The commission intends to go on meeting every month to determine new words and expressions that must bite the bullet. Hopefully, it will be able to get a hold of a lot more of the rascals before they do any real damage. Really though, what a funny mob these French are. To my own hopelessly Anglo-Saxon way of thinking the whole idea of trying artificially to guide the ebb and flow of words and expressions between languages is ludicrous. It makes me want to look one of the Gallic word policemen right in the eye and expostulate, very loudly . . . *Ah! Ah! Ah! Ah!*

The English translation? *Ha! Ha! Ha! Ha!*

NO USE RUNNING OFF AN *ALICADOO*, GIVE HIM THE FLICK PASS

The alicadoo was such a citron, that each of us tried to give him the flick pass, but we just couldn't Dunkirk.

Every group of people who spend a large amount of time together engaged in much the same activity invariably develop their own shorthand language, and it certainly holds true for the Wallabies.

At present the Australian team is in Brisbane preparing for Sunday's Test against the United States. From there we go on a six-week tour of New Zealand where the language will no doubt evolve some more, taking on new words and phrases while perhaps dropping others.

At the moment though, some of the favourites of the Wallaby lexicon include:

Alicadoo An official of one or other of the Rugby Unions, usually replete with blazer and tie and invariably seen in packs. To be fair, alicadoos are more often than not good fellows, though they can occasionally turn your 'whisky on the rocks' into just straight whisky . . . by the time they've finished telling you about the try they scored back in 1956 in the northwest corner of Eden Park. No rugby federation on earth has more alicadoos than the French Federation, where whole battalions of blue-blazered alicadoos storm ashore and swarm all over every touring team at every stop.

Jowl Can be a noun or a verb, as in 'have a great jowl' or 'to jowl', but what it means is 'to eat'.

127

Kippage Sleep. As in 'I'm really glad we didn't have training this afternoon because I really needed the kippage'.

K her in the G Kick her in the guts. As in get the engine going, as in let's get the hell going.

Dunkirk To pull out. In scrum training, on those occasions when the front row collapses, one or other of the gentlemen with their dials in the dirt may be heard to grunt through the swirling dust 'Dunkirk', which means the players behind should stop pushing and hopefully help the front row out of their mess by pulling back on their jerseys. Off the field, 'Dunkirk' is similar to 'K her in the G' in meaning.

Dirties Of unknown origin. A 'dirty' is short for a 'dirt-tracker', one meaning of which is that on the day of the game the player is a reserve. It is also used for the players who form the second XV during a tour and who seem to have little chance of playing in the Test matches. A 'dirty-dirty', on the other hand, is a more extreme form of dirty—someone in the touring party who is neither playing nor reserving. Invariably these players feel pretty 'dirty' about this, as in 'unhappy', and, on reflection, perhaps that is the origin of the word.

Lousy bag This is the bag in which all the team's valuables, or 'lousies', are stored while the team is out playing. Again, of unknown origin.

Housekeeping This is a team management term for details that need to be attended to. A meeting for 'housekeeping' is a meeting to sign forms, organise flights, tickets for the game etc., and all the other myriad loose ends that must daily be attended to. For the record, the French also use 'housekeeping', or its French equivalent, *faire le menage*, as part of their lexicon, though for them it means something else entirely.

Housekeeping to the French means to clean out, or clean up, one's opposition, usually by means of the liberal use of one's fists.

Citron This arose out of the French tour (citron is French for lemon), and it means someone who is a real pain, who just won't leave you in peace and who you wish you could give the flick pass to.

Flick pass Of obvious origins, to give someone, or something, the 'flick pass' means to get rid of the person or a proposal, in the same manner that one executes a flick pass on the ball—quickly and with a minimum of fuss.

Maori sidestep A crushing shoulder charge performed on the field by a player in possession of the ball, which makes up in virility and vigour that which it might just possibly lack in subtlety and technique. It arises out of the perception that the Maoris generally prefer to run over opposing players than run around them.

To run off On the field, 'to run off' someone means to let another player take up the ball, absorb the crushing tackle and give you the ball with the wind in your hair just as he falls, taking out the defender. He has 'taken all the heat' as it were, while you have 'run off him' and he has put you 'through the gap'.

Off the field it means more or less the same thing except that its application is purely social. In a crowded bar after a game, one of the more homely forwards, on rare occasions maybe even a second-rower, may say to one of the fairer, more married members of the team, 'put me through the gap mate, I'm going to run off you all night long'.

Translated, this means 'you are good looking and married, while I am ugly, single, lonely and a long way from home. Please use all your wiles to attract this girl and then, just at the last moment, send her my way. Keep trying till you get it right.'

Yes, you're damn right that a few of us are absolutely *outraged* at this nakedly sexist and chauvinistic sort of behaviour and have done everything possible to stamp it out. But what can you do? We're only footballers, after all.

GRUNT-MAN OUSTS PLAYMAKER IN LINE-BALL DECISION

For the hell of it, let's talk about words and phrases. Every year for the past few yonks, the various sports come up with new ones. Some fade quickly, others endure. Still others receive the ultimate accolade: carried off on the shoulders of raiding business troops, back to offices all over the land where 'team players', 'line-ball decisions' and 'selling the dump' suddenly become all the go.

Between the sports themselves there is also no little amount of exchange (to wit, tennis's original unforced error now has quite universal currency) though often something gets lost in the translation.

Rugby Union players, for example, have long been under the impression that ice-hockey players are always saying to each other 'Let's get the puck outta here'. But I checked recently and that is not so. They say 'let's go' like everybody else.

The point of all this? There is no point particularly, other than it amuses me and helps pass the time while sitting in this rugby World Cup camp watching endless videos of England and Wales. (Actually I love it, really I do.) Often the words describe concepts and as the word gains currency, so too the concept. (Or maybe the chicken came before the egg—I don't know.) A few years back, the Rugby League *playmaker* suddenly emerged. This was the team's linchpin, around which much of its attack would revolve. As soon as the word appeared, much of League analysis seemed to rely on it. Would Balmain beat Parramatta? Invariably, the expert opinion would be that a lot depended on how their two playmakers, Ben Elias and Peter Sterling, fared. There still are playmakers around of course, but somehow we don't seem to hear as much of them.

This year, the guys who are getting all the press are the impact players. If Johnny Bloggs is an impact player, it is that he is sure to have an 'impact' on the game if you throw

131

him into the breach. In this sense, an impact usually means either a try or the creation thereof.

Scott Gourley, when he played Union, was a classic impact player in that once or twice a game he could be counted on to do something extraordinary, which would frequently result in a try. Much as he now does in League. But he was not what the New Zealanders call a *grunt-man*. For them, the grunt-man is the guy who does all the selfless and anonymous work, like tackling, pushing, mauling, rucking. Actually, you know, the description sounds a lot like myse . . . no, never mind.

Of course, without at least a few grunt-men the impact player cannot bloom, and in return the grunt-men need the impact players to turn their work into points. The concept of the grunt-man has not yet crossed the creek from New Zealand but, for what it's worth, it gets my vote as a really thuper thuper phrase.

In French, the vogue sports phrase of the moment in football is *Le leaderrrr*. (Not actually spelt like that, but that's how they pronounce it.) They've taken the word of obvious English origin and turned it into a paramount concept.

Le leaderrrr is not necessarily the captain, and frequently isn't, but he's the guy who can be counted on to get the other guys' mustard up. By his tackles, his rampaging charges, his generally aggressive play, he is figuratively the guy who is first out of the trenches waving his arm in the classic *'follow me'* fashion.

The French wisdom is that without *un leader* a football team may as well not turn out, no matter what skill they might have on board. And in the US, the big word of the moment, to judge from the wire services, is a *gamer*. A gamer is one who may not be the strongest player, the most skilled, or with the most flair, but, hell, he or she knows how to win a game of whatever it is. Their ability lies not in the way they hit the ball or make the tackle, or throw the dart, but somehow in the way they are able to choose the way to play the game so as to win it.

A good example of a gamer might be former French tennis Open winner Michael Chang who, the pundits say, is way higher in the rankings than his technical ability would normally place him. So that's about it. The rugby videos are almost over now. England look great, Wales look terrible.

LOCKS AND LOAFERS AND OTHER FLIM-FLAM

My friend Flim has got this very sensitive medical condition—so sensitive it can only be named inside the privacy of the following parentheses. (Flim's got a black hole in her brain. One that ruthlessly sucks in and destroys even the most rudimentary sporting knowledge.)

It's very odd. And it's not just that Flim doesn't care about sport. She doesn't care about international politics either, but she knows who Francois Mitterrand and Brian Mulroney are. For my part, I may not care anything at all about classical music but I certainly know what a truly great composer Michelangelo was.

But as all-consuming as the black hole in Flim's head is, it has still not been able to destroy all the rugby terminology with which it's being bombarded as the World Cup tournament gains momentum.

Though her intellectual curiosity on matters sporting is zilch, some of the curious terms employed in rugby have lately tickled her fancy—to the point where she can be moved to paroxysms of laughter whenever she hears a commentator say something to the effect of 'and the loosehead prop has gone the blind side, only to be bundled into touch'.

But actually, it's not that funny. Rugby is a very, very serious business, and high merriment like that only confuses the issue of what is an important sporting event more than likely to bring the game greater international glory.

So, for all the Flims out there, here are a few basic rugby definitions, with which it will hopefully be possible to understand what is going on. First, the game itself.

Rugby is a neanderthal sort of game with the barest of late second millennium veneers painted over the top of it. The basic scheme is to move a piece of inflated leather up-field against the spirited resistance of those who are not only sworn to stop you, but are also trying to gain territory too. Add water, blood, mud, and mix.

The backs: rugby backs can be identified because they generally have clean jerseys and identifiable partings in their hair. It's a long story as to why this is so, but suffice to say that come the revolution, the backs will be the first to be lined up against the wall and shot for living parasitically off the work of others.

The forwards: these are the gnarled and scarred creatures who have a propensity for running into and bleeding all over each other. Their job is to get the ball so the backs can get the glory.

The coach: can be identified because every now and then the camera will flash to a bloke sitting in the stands who will either look like the cat that swallowed the canary or more likely have the demeanour of the said canary—as he contemplates the jaws of hell which are always open before him if his team loses.

The scrum: this is where the two sets of eight forwards push against each other with the ball in the middle, to make what the literary folk refer to as 'the beast with sixteen backs'.

The loose-head: the left-hand side of the scrum.

The tight-head: the right-hand side of the scrum. The way to remember this is that 'tight' rhymes with 'right'.

The blind side: that side of the field where there is least defence. (It's actually a lot more complex than that, but for Flim's benefit, this will suffice.)

The ruck: an informal scrum. More or less a mobile catfight for humans.

The maul: like a ruck except the ball is not on the ground so much as right in the middle of the catfight.

Chip kick: a little kick over the head of the opposition which the kicker performs with the intention of regathering. Generally, it is accepted that rugby players should refrain from chip kicks unless they have the happy conjunction of having 'Mark' for a first name and 'Ella' for a second name, because nineteen times out of twenty, chip kicks go wrong. But the backs love chip kicks regardless, because one of the special joys of their life is to waste the ball the forwards have worked so hard to win.

The five-eighth (outside-half): is between the half-back and full-back (get it?). With the No. 10 on his back, he is also more often than not the smoothest looking bloke on the field. You see, the 'selectors' know that just before kick-off, when the opposition lines up against their team, they will be looking for two things: has the team got big, gnarled second-rowers, and has it got a good looking five-eighth? A good-looking, unscarred five-eighth is scary to opposing teams because this means he must be so twinkle-toed and deft of foot he has been able to escape the ministrations of his enemies to date, and will more than likely be able to do so again on this day. Selectors pick their five-eighths accordingly. So it is one of rugby's little paradoxes that while, for an opposition team, 'ugly' can be terrifying in a second-rower, 'beauty' can be even more horrifying in a five-eighth.

Selectors: as a race, are low-down mongrel dogs. They nevertheless have the task of deciding who goes in the team.

Finally, Flim wanted a few answers to these questions. 'Who is this bloke fatty loafer and how come with a nick-name like that he got to be an international rugby player?' So help me God, but I think she was serious. His name is Peter Fatialofa and he happens to be the captain of the Western Samoan team which did so well in this tournament.

'Why do you boys like to play these games in the first place? What is so attractive about running into each other and frequently splitting your head open?' Hard to say really. But to put it in literary terms it's something like this. Remember that marvellous scene in *Henry V*, where Henry and a few hundred English soldiers are gathered in the valley as several thousand French troops are about to fall upon them? Then Henry V gathers the troops around him and offers these immortal lines, one of the great prematch speeches of our time . . . 'We few, we happy few, we band of brothers. For he today that sheds his blood with me shall be my brother.'

Well, in this modern era of Sensitive New Age Guys, compulsory seat belts and sorghum wheat grains for breakfast, rugby is one of the last bastions where you can still get the magnificence of that feeling—all for the price of a little light barbarism. But, after all, what's a little barbarism between friends?

'How does the offside rule work?' Uh, yes, good question. That is to say . . . it's like this . . . the ball's here and the players are here and . . . and . . . oh, forget it. The only people who can cite chapter and verse of the offside rule are the referees themselves. The rest of us just stagger round the best we know how, and occasionally note with mild surprise that we have infringed the offside rule. We know this because the referee is blowing his whistle and has his arm in the air to indicate a penalty which is then the signal for us to shake our head in total bewilderment that he could possibly put such an interpretation as that on our actions.

All that should keep my friend Flim busy for months.

THE TIPSTER'S GUIDE TO TOUCH FOOTBALL

They were all over Sydney again this weekend. Coming out of the ground, falling from the trees and suddenly materialising from thin air, on grassy verges all over the city. They are the tip (or touch) football players—men and women, boys and girls, and invariably a couple of dogs barking incessantly and getting in the way of everyone.

This is an activity that until a few years ago was confined mostly to a few footballers in the off-season and a few boarders on the oval after school, but it has now grown into a genuine and much-loved game of the masses.

How popular is it? It's so popular that my friend Flim, who a couple of months ago wouldn't have walked to the shop if she lived above it, is now something of a tip devotee. If Ms Anti-Sports herself is into it, I've gotta reckon the game has a future.

Of course Flim may still not know the difference between a cut-out pass and a block of flats . . . but she enjoys the sport, and is even finally starting to grasp why I like to play real football. The marvellous thing about tip is that all the teams, once they've been going for a while, give birth to the same basic types of people. People like . . .

The professional This is the guy who genuinely plays for one or other of the football clubs and already knows, dammit, the difference between a cut-out pass and a ham sandwich, and considers it really rather quite good of him to deign to show off his skills in such a lowly arena as this, but anyway . . .

Give me the ball! This type can usually be identified immediately: whenever someone drops the ball he can be seen to have his hands on his hips with his eyes rolling heavenwards.

The laughers Are the sworn enemy of the professionals. They have no idea how to catch, pass or run with the ball,

138

and every renewed failure on their part to do so sets them off into new paroxysms of laughing, contrasted to the rather stoic suffering silence of their team-mates. The professionals, invariably, can just barely control themselves from yelling at the laughers: 'Listen, you morons! Get the hell off the field so we can play.' Generally the rest of the team come to a consensus not to give laughers the ball under any circumstances.

The tip apostle A Mormon missionary in your living room should be such a pain. As opposed to most of the tip players who don't take it all that seriously, this guy is obsessed with the sport, and can often be heard to opine: 'You know, I think this game is every bit as hard as real football.' (Of course it's not as hard, you dummy, that's the whole point. In tip, you get all the pleasure of running with the ball in your hands without having to go to training three or four nights a week, or getting your head split open on the weekend.)

The quiet achiever Makes the hard yards, does the defence, hares across the field in cover and is rarely heard to squeak. The quiet achiever in a tip team is gold, pure gold . . . and almost as rare.

The dreamer He's got the leadership of Wally Lewis, the acceleration of Laurie Daley, the goosestep of Campese and the sheer imaginative power of Walter Mitty. No sooner does he step onto the tip field than he becomes a demon. The thing he hates most in this world is to execute a simple run forward and pass to the left or right. Nooooo. Too easy. What he likes is to twirl the ball behind his back, between his legs, dummy left, dummy right, and then attempt a cut-out pass right across field in an attempt to nail the blind winger on the burst, which—if it worked—would set up one of the great tip tries of our time. It never does work, of course, and the ball is invariably lost to the opposing team through his outrageous plays, none of which fazes him in the least.

The talker His mouth opens and shuts at more or less the same rate as his little legs pound, and he can be counted on to give a constant stream of directions. 'Go left. Go right. Get back five. Up in a line. Up in a line, I say.' Nobody actually listens to him, of course, but you just let him go on like that regardless. Some people can't play unless they're constantly shouting, and you should realise this and let him have his head. Or his mouth.

Putting together the whole thing is a lot of fun, and according to figures from the Bureau of Statistics, tip is approximately 1232.5 times more fun than mere jogging.

8 THE HOW-TO OF RUGBY

RHYTHM? IT MUST BE IN THE CHOW MEIN

In the mathematics of sport they were two statistical kings, meeting for the first time in an Auckland Chinese restaurant. On my left, helping himself to the chicken chow mein, Sir Richard Hadlee—the greatest wicket-taker of all time, with no fewer than 431 Test notches carved into his bowling arm. On my right, with the won ton soup, Michael Lynagh—Wallaby five-eighth and world record-holder for points scored in Test matches, at the time on 542 points.

In the presence of two such greats, the overwhelming duty of any self-respecting sports journalist was obvious— to identify, isolate, and if possible, bottle the common features of their greatness before sprinkling it liberally all over oneself at appropriate moments. Unfortunately, there were no self-respecting sports journalists to be seen, so I had to fill the breach. Right away it was obvious, on the strength of knowing Lynagh for eight years and Hadlee for eight minutes, that they have similar personalities. 'Self-contained' is the word that springs to mind. Both extremely likable in a Brian Henderson sort of way, though, like Hendo, not the sort of person you'd be inclined to slap on the back in the classic 'hail fellow well met' fashion unless you knew them well.

Another word that springs to mind, while on the subject, is 'noneffusive'—one suspects that that which is in their hearts and souls is not necessarily evident on their faces. Ergo, on this reckoning, perhaps the most crucial ingredient to go in the greatness bottle would be some of those famed still waters that run deep. But enough of this mashed potato.

Hadlee says the four things that he has based his magnificent bowling career on are rhythm, hate, off stump and Dennis Lillee. Lynagh says the two things he has based his munificent goal-kicking career on are rhythm and slow.

You got me. I tried to slip it by you, but you got me fair and square. The intersecting point of their greatness is rhythm. You will also have no doubt noted that there was no other point where they could have intersected because, given the difference of their disciplines, there is no way Noddy Lynagh could always aim for the off goal-post, nor could he summon hate in his heart for the uprights, nor could he in times of trial ask himself 'what would Dennis Lillee do in this situation?'

For that matter it would be a contradiction in terms for the great fast bowler Hadlee to remind himself constantly to be as slow as possible. So to rhythm. And it's very simple. Both agree the essence of their considerable skills—which is to send balls exactly where they have to go—relies primarily on perfecting the rhythm immediately before the ball is released. Not to do it this way one time and that way another time, but to always do it exactly the same way.

By keeping the outer parameters of their rhythms as close together on the spectrum as possible, the variations of where the ball will end up are equally tightened—in Hadlee's case to the width of a five-cent piece. As Hadlee says: 'It's like a golfer hitting a drive or a tennis player serving a ball. If you get the rhythm of the action right, the rest will take care of itself. If the action is always the same the ball will always end up in the same spot. It sounds simple and self-evident, but it is the essence of the skill.'

And if you need any further help on your Emulation of Greatness program, both these greats seemed to hoe into the chow mein . . .

WELCOME TO FIRST GRADE, LADS!

Even as we speak, there are perhaps 25 or so of them out there. Young blokes picked to play in their debut first-grade rugby union game tomorrow. First Grade! They've made it. So congratulations.

For what it's worth, here are a few tips about how to get along.

1   Be on the quiet side of things for at least your first few weeks in the team. For new chums, a certain silent resilience is generally regarded as the appropriate air to affect within the team, as is respect for your older team-mates and the opportunity that has been given you in equal measure. Things will loosen up in short order, but that should come from them initially, not you.

2   Come the day, expect to be as nervous as a hedgehog trespassing in a balloon factory. Particularly if you're a forward, outright fear about the coming battle is a rite of passage.

3   And rightly so. In the middle of the game it'll happen like this: you'll be minding your own business, fringing on the side of a ruck, when some mean mongrel dog who's played for years will have lined you up from 20 metres out, and will hit you so hard with his shoulder he'll send you cartwheeling backwards over and over.

   Your head will hit the ground every time as you turn, and the thought may very well occur to you that 'if this is first grade, let me out!'.

   Don't worry. It's just his way of saying 'welcome to first grade' and it's nothing serious. Besides, it gets better. While the top grade is a big step up from colts or schoolboys or second grade or wherever it is you've come from, it doesn't take long to adapt.

4   At the end of the game, always be sure to go up and shake the referee's hand and look him in the eye as you

say something to the effect of 'thank you very much Sir, good game'. Say this even if the ref hasn't had a good game, because he'll appreciate more than ever a friendly word and . . .

Here's the rub. Ten minutes later, when this same ref sits down to award best and fairest points, he'll very possibly remember you with affection. No kidding. Even when you've played like a dog, it's still possible to squeeze a point or two out of them and you'll show up better than expected when the end of season tally is announced.

5 After the game, if perchance you find yourself talking to a rugby journalist, avoid at all costs mouthing empty banalities about how you thought 'rugby was the winner on the day' or 'it was the bounce of the ball that decided it'.

Say something, anything, but don't be boring. If you want to get your name in the paper, and let's face it, you do, saying something interesting helps.

6 Enjoy it. Sure it's first grade and sure it's serious, but don't become so serious about it all that you don't have time to lie around on the tackle bags after training is over and talk about the events of the day—just as you should always stay back after the game to have a drink with the other team.

7 Through it all, never doubt that you're part of some-thing magnificent. If you get to tackle Farr-Jones on Saturday, don't forget that in the past he's tackled Jeremy Guscott who's tackled Serge Blanco who's tack-led Paul McClean who's tackled John Hipwell who's tackled Ken Catchpole . . . and so on. BOOM! One tackle on Farr-Jones and you're connected up—world-wide and right back through the ages.

And whether or not you go on to representative honours it doesn't really matter. The pleasures of grade rugby are plentiful.

Maybe ten years from now you'll be drinking tea on your front porch on an autumn afternoon, and you'll see some guy walk past who you used to play football against for years and years—a really nippy five-eighth for example, who you always dreamed of creaming but you could never get close enough to the brute to do it.

But no matter, you'll talk for a little while about old games you played and other players and what they're up to these days, and presently he'll go back to walking his dog, but as you go back to your tea you'll reflect that all over Sydney Town there are guys that you've played with and against, and you'll be glad you played the game.

SOMETIMES, ALL YOU'RE FIT FOR IS REST

It's rising that time of year when amateur footballers begin to stir, shake off the lethargy of summer daze, and gird themselves for the coming winter campaigns. The professionals have already been at it for months. Fitness: they need to start stocking up now. But where do you get it in most copious quantities? The swimming pool? The track? The road? The gym? And how frequently and how long should you exercise for optimum effect?

Each year the theories vary as new fitness fashions go in and out of vogue. Notwithstanding the invariable belief of coaches that their own program-of-the-moment is writ large on a tablet just descended from heaven, there are no absolutes about which kind of exercises are best to get fit quickly. But there are at least some parameters between which the training should fall.

That repository of all sports science wisdom, the American College of Sports Medicine, recently re-released its position paper on how to achieve optimum physical fitness—making several changes from its 1978 study. As reported in the *New York Times*, the basic recommendations, suitable for everyone from Carl Lewis down to Fred McGhurkin-Squirter, were:

- Training should be carried out three to five days a week.
- Optimum efficiency is gained by an intensity level of 60–90 per cent of maximum heart rate, or 50–80 per cent of maximum oxygen use.
- Top athletes, but not the general public, should exercise at their maximum heart-rate level for at least 20–60 minutes each session.
- Where a program calls for aerobic work, weight training should not be considered an aerobic exercise. According to the paper: 'One set of eight to twelve repetitions of

148

eight to ten exercises that condition the major muscle groups should be performed at least two days a week.'

Not that weight training is downgraded. On the contrary, it enjoys new prestige as a crucial part of any serious fitness program. According to the report, the inclusion of weight training on the list is 'perhaps the most significant finding in the twelve years between the publication of the position papers'.

The paper also noted, using the 1978 study as a base, that training at 60–90 per cent of maximum heart-rate for 20–60 minutes was increased from a minimum of fifteen minutes, and intensity levels were raised by 15–30 per cent. Viewed from this end of the globe, this information seems to fit in well with the growing body of local sporting opinion that good physical fitness training is intense, punctuated by a good amount of rest in preparation for the next effort.

NEW PAIN, MORE GAIN

Not so many moons ago, the trainer of every rugby team in captivity could be counted on to eternally scream 'No pain, no gain!' at his charges over and over again as he put them through torturous drills designed to make them suffer physically for as long as possible. This would get them 'fit', it was deemed.

And rightly so. But such a simple formula for fitness for any mainstream sport is no longer the universal way. Nowadays, at the top level of rugby and other sports, although the principle of 'no pain, no gain' is still sacred, it has been comprehensively refined.

In the modern era of sport, you must have specific kinds of pain at specific times, with a specific amount of recovery time. And after your pains, your gains will be precisely measured to determine just what sort of pain it is best to go to next.

It sounds a lot more gruesome than it actually is. But what results is that we muddied oafs, and many other athletes, are now mingling freely with studious types holding clipboards covered with odd-shaped graphs. Science has arrived on the training field, and also influences what and when we eat. . .

The common wisdom used to be that a blood-red steak was the best meal during training periods, as well as before matches. No doubt based on the atavistic assumption that something so sturdy and strong as a cow would be certain to give us strength, we tucked into the blood-reds with gusto. Now, it's widely known that carbohydrates is the correct type of sport food to eat, but there's still an encyclopedia's worth of information available beyond that. Personally, I miss the steaks, but that's another story.

In the past two months, the Wallabies have had two weekend camps, where apart from engaging in a lot of training sessions and precise physical testing, we have also had to take pen and notebook in hand to gather the state-of-the-art wisdom from a variety of experts paraded past us. They are the support staff of the Wallabies bid for the World Cup 1991—the people Australian coach Bob Dwyer invariably refers to as 'the best support staff of any of the teams competing for the World Cup'.

Their message is not easy to absorb. All are experts in their physiological fields, and as such have the usual academic propensity to use words with a ridiculous number of syllables in them, but if you force their arms far enough up between their shoulder blades they can be persuaded to turn it into common English. Their combined wisdom has an application far wider than just rugby.

Strength training (Brian Hopley)

Hopley is a Master of Applied Science in exercise physiology and the manager of the Manly Rugby League Club Fitness Centre to boot. In that capacity, he works daily on the task of increasing the strength of sportspeople. For strength training, he constructs a pyramid image for players to work off. At the base of the pyramid is sufficient bulk.

Without it, a person, particularly one in a contact sport, can be severely limited in reaching their potential. As Hopley tells it, bulk is a little like a vase in which you can later pour in strength. The bigger the vase, the more strength it can contain, though it is possible to have a big vase that is essentially empty of strength.

In the case of rugby, an example of a football player adding bulk to realise his potential is grand slam Wallaby Steve Cutler, who only secured his Test spot after following a long program to increase his bulk. Before him, famous Wallaby Rob Hemming achieved similar success by adding bulk; after him, emerging Wallaby David Dix is currently pursuing the same basic program. To increase bulk by using weights, the essential plan is to do high repetition. When doing bench presses for example, you should choose a weight that you will be able to lift off your chest about twelve times. After you have completed the first set, you must rest a little and then do another one. Only work one muscle group at a time, the basic idea being to overload work on the muscle.

Body builders who really get into this sort of stuff talk about 'going for the burn' which means working the muscle until you get a burning sensation. This is the build-up of lactic acid in the muscles, a by-product of the work you have done and, for some reason way beyond my capacity to understand, it makes your muscles grow.

For most effective bulking you should work out four to five times a week pre-season. Once you have sufficient bulk, then you can move on to developing strength.

Strength To fill the vase of your bulk with strength, you must increase the amount of weights you are working with and thus lower the amount of repetitions to four to six maximum. As you get stronger, of course, you increase the amount of weights you use and three to four good sessions a week is optimal.

Power At the peak of the pyramid, and after you have the base of sufficient bulk and the strength overlay, comes the power. Power is strength divided by time, and for the rugby player, as for any other athlete, it is of paramount importance. Illustrative of this point is that when Ben Johnson or Carl Lewis run the 100-metre sprint in under ten seconds, they're really only in physical contact with the ground for a few seconds.

It's for those split seconds they are in contact with the ground that their explosive power must be fully expressed, and it is this very explosiveness which separates them from the also-rans. Ergo, after the bulk and strength parts of your program are in place, you can now work on explosive power.

Hopley says this can be done in two basic ways in the gym. Either have a low weight and do 23 explosive repetitions; or have high weight and do three to four reps as explosively as you can. Of course with a high weight you won't be able to do it really fast, but the important thing is to do it as fast as possible. Your explosive power will be enhanced.

Prevention of injuries Hopley also notes that apart from the advantages of weight training for the development of power, it also aids in minimising the risk of injury. For the footballer, it is a particularly good idea to do a lot of 'leg curls' and 'leg extensions' so as to strengthen the muscles supporting the knee. This is because in the whole body the knee is the greatest point of vulnerability for footballers.

General conditioning (David Jenkins)

A lecturer at the University of Queensland who has just completed his PhD in exercise physiology, Jenkins's specialty is high-intensity exercise. To achieve ideal fitness he constructs a similar pyramid image to Hopley's, though with only two basic levels to it. At the base of the pyramid is 'cardiovascular fitness'—in English, endurance fitness. This is the ability of the body to work at medium to high intensity over a long period of time. It is developed by regularly raising the pulse rate of your heart up to 75 per cent of its maximum and keeping it there for a bare minimum of twenty minutes, and ideally for at least half an hour. Running and swimming are the most common ways of achieving this high pulse rate and it has the added benefit of promoting fat loss which Jenkins says is 'vital if the mobility of the footballer is to be improved'.

When a high degree of cardiovascular fitness has been attained it is time to move on to the second tier of the pyramid, which is anaerobic fitness—in English again, training without oxygen. This means a lot of short sharp activity, like sprints, which will acclimatise the body to continue performing even when there is little oxygen in the bloodstream.

Endurance training is not ignored in this phase, but rather enters a maintenance period. In football, the point of anaerobic exercises is to mimic the conditions which the player will soon experience in the game, and as the season approaches the amount of recovery time allowed in anaerobic sessions should be cut down. Needless to say, the wider the base of the cardiovascular fitness, the greater will be the anaerobic capacity that can be overlaid on it.

Diet (Holly Frail)

A professional sports dietitian, Frail has worked with the Wallabies for the past two years and has closely studied the dietary needs of sportspeople. In point form, her advice can be best summarised as follows.

- While in full training it is better to have six smaller meals throughout the day than three large ones. This maximises the energy available for both training and recovery.
- Carbohydrates should be the staple part of your diet. More than 60 per cent carbohydrate is recommended as optimal, though, when analysed, most footballers get by on less than 50 per cent.
- It is very important to have some carbohydrate intake, in liquid or solid form, within 30–60 minutes after completing the training exercise. This promotes the most rapid recovery of glycogen stores in the muscles— glycogen being, as I understand it, a substance from which our muscles draw energy.
- It is almost impossible to drink too much water. No macho nonsense here troops. Drink it, Freddy. The body performs at its best only when it is fully hydrated.
- For those sportspeople trying to lose weight prior to their season, it is still important that they consume enough kilojoules so as to be able to follow a full training program. However, the evening meal should be particularly reduced, and it is ideal that the rest of your intake be done before training, so it can be easily burnt off. Avoid fatty foods like you do the bathroom scales after Christmas dinner.
- For those unbelievably lucky ones trying to gain weight for the football season, it's particularly important you ingest food every two or three hours throughout the day. Increase the intake of high-energy drinks (eg milk drinks, fruit juices) and high-energy foods (eg dried fruit and nuts, healthy fruit-type buns'/cakes/ scones/ muffins, yoghurts, extra sandwiches, cereals, larger

servings of starchy vegetables/rice/pasta, etc.) with and between meals.

- There is no perfect meal to have before performance, but generally a high carbohydrate, low fat meal should be eaten at least three to four hours before kick-off, and be accompanied by a high fluid intake. An example of this meal would be pasta with a tomato paste or low-fat sauce. Rice is good, as is fruit, cereal, and toast with honey.

So, all set? Take a look at yourself now. Your shoulders would do justice to a piano mover. Your legs were carved by Michelangelo. Your stomach looks like the proverbial washboard and you could run a marathon with a Kenyan. You are now ready to go . . . unless you are a rugby player. For you, there remains only one problem. Your head, my man, your head. We've still got to do something about it. Let's talk to a sports psychologist.

Psychology (Dr Ian Lynagh, clinical sports psychologist)

Each rugby player has an optimum level of 'arousal' when playing. 'Arousal' refers to the degree of intensity of physical and psychological energy. If the arousal level is too low ('Yawn, what's on telly tonight?'), a lethargic, under-powered, uncoordinated performance results. If too high ('WE'RE GOING TO TEAR THEIR HEADS OFF!'), erratic, inaccurate, behaviour lacking fine motor coordination is the outcome. To increase arousal levels when low, it is often useful to pump-prime the adrenalin by engaging in sharp physical activity together with rousing self-talk and mental rehearsal of the tasks that are about to be performed. To lower arousal levels it is useful to consciously breathe slowly and deeply and practise calming self-talk. It would also help if you stopped banging your head on the wall.

So, finally we really are all set for the game. Now, GO GET 'EM! Sorry, that should read, 'Now, go get 'em.'

THE SEASON TO END REASON: LET'S TOUR

It's that time of year again. The days grow longer, the birdies start chirping merrily in the sky, the flowers begin to bloom, and the fancies of young men and women everywhere turn gradually from their winter pursuits . . . from their footballs, hockey-sticks and what-nots . . . and start to focus in on the very essence of life itself. Touring.

End-of-season tours to foreign climes are the highlight of the year for many sporting clubs, and even as we speak, money is being raised by a variety of methods to pay for air tickets, accommodation, and trains, planes, buses and cars for sporting outfits all over the country.

But how best to go about it? With the help of Everald Compton, the foremost professional fundraiser in Australia, here are a few clues:

- First, identify your 'constituency'. Who, specifically, are those people who have goodwill towards your sporting organisation?
- Now, analyse their tastes, likes, weaknesses, peccadillos and prejudices, to determine how best to turn goodwill into *cash*. (I know this is a bit cold-bloodedly Machiavellian, but do you want to tour or not?)
- Know that, in the sporting context, it is not enough to simply ask your supporters for money. You are not an inherently noble cause like the National Heart Foundation, and people won't automatically reach for their wallet or purse when you ask. To get the cash, you must provide some form of entertainment, diversion or tangible return for their money. Ideally, come up with something that will not only tap your supporters' wallets, but those of their friends too.
- A classic example of this is Sydney Uni Football Club, which is holding a fundraising campaign to go on a tour to Ireland. They went through the same process.

156

Who are the main supporters of their club? They are the students themselves. What is a particular weakness of university students? They fancy like mad their own INCREDIBLY WIDE general knowledge. Thus? Uni held a 'trivia night', with prizes for tables of people with the proven widest general knowledge and charged them all $30 to come in. On the night, they were beating them away from the door with a stick—not just the rugby followers, but also all their smartie friends. They raised something like $15 000 on the night from the 600 people who came.

- When you turn to the old tried and true fundraiser of raffles, forget chook raffles. Think BIG. The proceeds of even a good-sized chook raffle would be unlikely to pay your collective departure tax these days. Instead, why don't you, for example, say to the airline which is flying your 30 people to Europe or wherever: 'Look, schmuckos, we're putting sixty grand of airfares into your coffers, so can't you at least kick in a free return airfare for two to Hawaii?' If they've any sense they'll buckle. And if they don't, then find another airline.

- Another way to make money is to produce a small magazine-type publication with photos from your season, player profiles, messages from your president and perhaps an article or two about how, when all is said and done, there are only really two types of people in the world: those who play for your club and those who wish they played for your club. That sort of thing . . . then sell advertising space to local businesses and distribute the magazine to all your supporters. One well-known amateur organisation raised $40 000 doing this last year.

Two other points in general.

- It is important to keep winning your games. Goodwill goes to winners, as does money.
- When you've got the fundraising going, the people who must have their shoulders to the wheel are not just an isolated committee of three or four, but rather all those

157

people who are most to benefit from the proceeds, the players themselves. In the raffle, for example, nobody gets on the plane until they've sold at least ten raffle books. Got all that? Good. Now get out there and FLEECE 'EM. Happy touring.

So, you loved the World Cup. Finally you figured out what the rugga buggas have been on about all these years and now you'd like to start your own rugby club . . . Welcome aboard. You've got about six months before the next domestic season starts, which should be plenty of time. First, get yourself a field.

Don't be fooled by the fact that you will henceforth be known as being a part of 'grassroots rugby'. This is not because anyone actually expects to find any grass roots beneath their feet when they come to play you. Plain dirt is fine, though it probably should have at least a few token tufts of grass here and there.

Now you need a coach. This guy has got to really, absolutely, and I mean totally, *love* the game. 'Greater love of rugby hath no man than that he will agree to coach' and it is a fair bet that his life will become absolute hell from the moment he accepts the position. To prepare him, make sure your coach announces preseason training sometime around the middle of January. No one will come, of course, which is the very point of the exercise. It's important your coach gets used to getting disappointed early, otherwise he'll never make it through the long season.

A treasurer. A good rule of thumb is that to make a decent treasurer, be it for a rugby club or the nation, you need to have one of the names of the twelve apostles. Look for a guy called John or James or Peter or something like that. He should be a fairly serious, sober, long-suffering sort of bloke and it would really help if, in his own life, he somehow managed to feed and clothe a family of four on the basic wage. Steer a mile wide of guys with nicknames like Flash Larry, Elvis or Lothario. They make good five-eighths but lousy treasurers.

Now for the players. The best way to get these is to start scouring the pubs in your area. We'll start from the bottom up, so let's presume your club is going to have three grades. The most essential ingredient for a good third-grade is personalities. Really livewire sort of blokes who love the game, are not much good at it . . . but that doesn't matter because their main role is to be keepers of the club soul. They should have names like Louie, Jacko, Thommo . . . that sort of thing. At least two of them should be absolutely legendary for some late-night feat of the recent past.

This should be constantly referred to by others in the team, not necessarily explicitly, but along the lines of 'what about the time Jacko . . . !?!?!' and the sayer should be unable to finish for all the other guys in the team falling around laughing, digging each other in the ribs and giving each other knowing looks. Whatever it was that Jacko did, it should get better and better with every passing month.

For the second grade, you need slightly more serious types with a bit of ambition. Seriousness can be measured by smoking less than two packets a day, sobriety on the day of the game and, occasionally . . . just very occasionally . . . actually turning up to training.

Props. Look around where the motorbike blokes hang out. If you can find a couple of blokes called Igor, Nutcracker or something like that, then they're exactly the ones you're looking for. In fact, any guys with nicknames like these would fit well into your forward pack.

As to the backs, what would be really terrific would be if they had last names like Campese, Farr-Jones or Lynagh but you're probably setting your hopes a bit high there, so don't make that an absolute precondition. Instead, look for smaller guys with discernible parts in their hair, shirts neatly tucked into their trousers and no known criminal records. These are the sort of guys who generally make the best backs.

Finally, you'll need some barflys. These shouldn't be too hard to find. A bare minimum of five or six of these should be sprinkled liberally around the bar where you drink at and they should at all times have only the very slenderest of holds on sobriety.

Furthermore, and this is most crucial, they should constantly express at the top of their voice their opinion about all matters concerning the club. The subtext of everything they say must be 'if only I was president/coach/captain then everything would be going about ten times better'. There you go, that's more or less the basic ingredients. Add water—or beer, if you must—and enjoy.

THE BIG WET

It had been raining for weeks. Gazing morosely from his penthouse balcony, Australia's foremost astronomer was bored. From the grey gloom above to the grey sprawl below, nothing appeared to be happening. Yet something had caught his eye. Way, way in the distance. Distractedly taking up his powerful home telescope, he focused on it. He gasped in surprise. Was it possible? Before him he saw a scene that looked to be a re-enactment of man's first moments on the planet. First the boiling mud. Then the gradual movement. Finally the first primeval man, rising violently from the sludge, blindly trotting his first tentative steps forward, then being knocked over by the second primeval man coming equally blindly the other way. What could it possibly be? Then he twigged. It was a football game. Which explained some things. He continued watching for the rest of the game, always pondering the same question: 'Could there possibly be any intelligent life down there?'

As a matter of fact, yes. And despite appearances, the muddier it is the more need for intelligent play there is. Football in the mud can be as different from football in the dry as a New South Welshman is from a Queenslander, as a sophisticate from a redneck. So, three coaches from their respective football codes ran through the tactics and techniques they would use when in the mud:

Bob Dwyer, Australian rugby coach

To win a rugby game you need to win the ball, keep it, and advance with it. This doesn't change in the mud but the method of doing it does.

To win the ball: In the scrum each player must have all his sprigs squarely grounded. When the ball is won, it should be channelled to the right-hand side of the lock. This keeps it as far as possible from the opposing half-back, who will pounce on any mistake. In the line-out, long throws are out, as are hard flat throws. Both have too large a margin for error.

To keep the ball: There are several things to do, but the most basic is to stay basic and cut out the fancy, high-risk stuff. If your margin for error in the dry, on a cut-out pass to your fullback is 'x', it is at least '3x' in the wet. Better to keep it simple. Equally, passes have to be a lot more 'lobby' to make it as easy as possible for the receiver to get his hand on the ball. As a general principle, the ball should be kept close to the forwards so as to clean up on the inevitable mistakes.

To advance the ball: The essence of this in the wet is to get the ball in front of the advantage line and to have the forwards running forward on to it from there. The best way to do this is to have one of three—the half-back, the five-eighth or the lock (the three closest to the advantage line)—take the ball up in short bursts. It is then easy for your forwards to run onto it and take it up, while it is murder for the opposition to get back, turn in the mud and stop the rot.

For the kicking game, chip kicks are out as they will not bounce up. Non-bounce will be an advantage though in box kicks because you know the ball is going to stay put when it lands and you can position the ball very precisely to your own advantage.

Bob Fulton, Australian rugby league coach

Generally, to win in the wet you need to base your game on three things: a good strategic kicking game, a strong chasing team and a strong defence. The more difficult it is to advance on the ground, the better idea it is to advance in the air. Thus the kicking game becomes doubly important to establish field position. The smarter coaches no longer have their kickers kicking for the line, but have them kick down-field, preferably to the open spaces.

From here you need a good strong chasing team to either pin the opposing player in his own in-goal, or at least cut down on the easy yardage he can make up-field. The chasers must come up hard and spread flat. The need for a particularly strong defence in the wet is because points and position come hard in the mud. Thus, it is even more imperative not to let through any cheap yardage or soft tries.

Another general principle to pursue in the wet is to be increasingly conservative the closer you are to your own line. That means to rarely spin the ball wide in your own 40 and basically have the forwards make the hard yardage. Absolutely no mistakes in close. In their quarter you can spin it wide if any breaks appear in their defence. As to techniques for holding on to the ball when you have it, this has largely been resolved now that the league is using wet-weather balls.

Ron Barassi, Australian Rules coach

The difference in the wet is mainly one of technique. Generally, you want to attempt shorter kicks and shorter hand passes. On the hand passes you must take particular care to hit the ball at the point where the four seams meet so it won't go slithering off. For receiving the ball it is doubly important to get in front of your opponent early, as the ball will be coming to you lower and there is less room to manoeuvre over the top of someone.

When taking the ball in the air, the fingers must be very tensed and the hands inclined more in the direction of the ball, to compensate for the ball's increased weight and slipperiness. On the half-volley, take particular care that your arm is closely parallel to your leg so as to form a 'wall', similar to a cricketer protecting his off-stump with the bat close to the leg.

A good way to warm up before the game is to put a ball in oily water and pass it around the changing room.

As an overall strategy, play basic football without the fancy stuff.

9 MISH-MASH

THE TOUGHEST POSITION: LEFT RIGHT OUT

Auckland: Daly, McCall, Campbell . . . The penny drops with the force of a thunder-clap between your ears and you stagger back to your lonely room, almost oblivious to the many consolatory pats on your back. Back to your nasty, zoo-like little room.

What sort of cretin would put carpets on the wall, anyway? And why didn't the moron at least have the brains to see how totally depressing such dim lighting would be when one of the hotel guests had just been dropped from the Test team? If only you had the interior decorator there; you would surely carpet him by punching his lights out. You have some slight malicious satisfaction of booking the four selectors in for optometry appointments for the next day, and suggest that they might like to try Coke bottles for lenses to be able to see the games better in future, but the pain remains. Not to mention the humiliation.

When you partially emerge from the fog of misery, you know it is time to observe a time-honoured ritual for such occasions. Thus, meeting with all your fellow deposed in a private room (where Test players are barred), you get down to some serious drinking, despairing and tearing into the selectors over what you all naturally perceive to be the insanity of their selection policies. The arguments on their side seem, of course, puerile by comparison, and you seriously wonder if there is any justice left in the world. Did any innocent clergyman, framed and convicted of the murder of one of his parishioners, ever feel so hard done by and bereft? You seriously doubt it.

The following day, when you get up after a solid night spent staring at the cracks in the ceiling, you don't want to believe that it's actually happened, but it has. It's so hoo-miliating. 'Rugby is a nonsense, but a serious nonsense,' someone once said. But when you're taking it seriously enough to play at this level, the 'nonsense' part doesn't ring true any more. It is serious, dammit, Goldilocks.

Your fall from grace is further manifested by the immediate change in the group dynamics of the Wallaby touring team. The thing is, you're no longer part of the XV. The Test Fifteen. Sure, to a man, your former Test teammates come up and quietly commiserate, but there is no changing the fact that now new loyalties are formed and you are no longer a part of them.

(By the way, did I mention somewhere in here that I hate life?)

In a touring party of 30 there is always an innate consciousness among you of who is in the Test team and who isn't, and there is no kidding yourself when you're out of it. Things have changed. And it's not just that you're not training at one end of the field while the Test team trains at the other. Also, in your daily life together, what used to seem like a faint but definite Rubicon between Test and non-Test players, now looks like the Grand Canyon.

It's quite simple. On this side are the Test players, who have the desired and cherished spots. On the other side are the non-Test players, who want the same spots. The Test players do battle side-by-side at the highest level, which inevitably binds them even tighter, while you are left out.

When the Test players run out on to the field and stand arm-in-arm to sing the national anthem—while you are left impotent in the stands—it's almost more than you can bear. Look, I can't go on. Life really stinks. Or did I mention that already?

YOU CAN'T CREATE A MASTERPIECE
WITH A SECOND-RATE CHISEL

*The rules of rugby have changed since this article was penned,
but I think the points on the referee remain valid. But then again,
I suppose I would . . .*

The sun was shining, the stands were packed, 30 of the
world's best footballers were ready to play like a German
oom-pah band, and millions of people were tuned in
worldwide to a game that was to be played right at the
very summit of world rugby. The All Blacks vs the Wallabies. Who won? Who knows.

Nominally, the All Blacks won the game 6–3, but in
terms of who was actually the better team, it's very hard
to say with any certainty. So very little rugby, with the ball
actually in play, occurred . . .

In a turn-around of the old cliche, Rugby Union was
the loser on the day. Start with the 80 minutes. Deduct
line-out-time. There were 28 of them, taking fifteen minutes. 80–15=65 minutes left. There were also 28 scrums,
taking another fifteen minutes. 65–15=50 minutes left. Penalties. There were *thirty-three* of the brutes taking 25 minutes including goal kicks. 45–20=25 minutes.

In fact, when you precisely calculate with a stopwatch
the amount of time played, there was twelve minutes sixteen seconds in the first half and twelve minutes 51 seconds
in the second half, bringing a grand total of 25 minutes
and seven seconds of actual play.

Result: one potentially great game destroyed. The most
damning figure in all that of course is the penalty count.
Thirty of the world's best players with a collective total of
some 400 years of rugby playing behind them and, with so
much at stake, they couldn't help themselves but to have
33 transgressions in 80 minutes? You're kidding. Either the

rules are too delicately balanced on their perches, if players of that calibre still can't help knocking them off, or more likely, there was a problem with the way the rules were interpreted.

The strong suspicion has got to be the latter. The referee, Scotsman Ken McCartney, blew it. And blew it and blew it and blew it, till his lungs fairly burst. A good football game has 30-parts player and one-part referee, while in this game it seemed the formula was reversed. Only occasional glimpses of rugby were to be seen through the refereeing extravaganza.

Good teams, of course, should be able to overcome bad referees and that is accepted. There has, for example, long been a laconic saying in the Wallabies that 'the five most useless things in the world are the Pope's balls and three cheers for the ref'. (Please don't send nasty letters about this, it's just a *joke*, okay? So lighten up.)

But the point is the ref was a problem for the game and not just the Wallabies. To steal a line from former Australian coach Dave Brockhoff, who once yelled at a player he was not happy with, 'I don't blame *you*, son, I blame the *selectors* who picked you!'—the same can be said to this referee.

No doubt Mr McCartney did his very best to referee to the very best of his ability and there is no suggestion he was anything other than sincere in his efforts. It took extraordinary courage to award the penalty to Australia, with 41 seconds to go, which might have won them the Bledisloe Cup. But he wasn't up to controlling such a game and it is not surprising.

As the fourth- or fifth-placed referee in Scotland there is every possibility that he is not among the top 30 in the world. And yet, under the current International Rugby Board system, he was given control of a match between the two best teams in the world.

But without a good referee the game cannot fly. The ref must create a good game, the same way that Michelangelo created the statue of David. 'Ol Mick started with a big block of marble and just carved away all those bits of rock that didn't look like David until he was left with the finished masterpiece. And the ref must do the same. He must start with the raw unshaped game and carve away all the rough ugly bits until he gets down to the really good part. But when he takes an automatic jack-hammer to it and blasts the whole thing out of existence, good and bad alike, the system that let him get even near the burgeoning masterpiece in the first place has got to be changed. Forthwith.

NOW THE BILLS WON'T BE LEFT TO GLORY

Some years ago the great French Rugby Union No. 8 Jean-Luc Joinel explained to *moi* why he had taken a job which, though lucrative, would inevitably mean the end of his Test career. 'When my son will come to me and say he's hungry, I will not have to say to him, "Sorry *mon fils*, there's no food in the refrigerator, but come and have a look at all my Test jerseys one more time." '

Lest the case be overstated, Jean-Luc was far from poverty-stricken, but the point he made was valid: glory alone pays no bills. Or at least it didn't. The International Rugby Board has announced there is to be a long-awaited liberalisation of rugby's strict amateurism laws—effectively allowing players to convert a few of their glory chips into cash. Though players will receive no direct over-the-table payments for playing the game, such things as paid after-dinner speaking, product endorsements and personal appearances for money are now to be formally allowed. Good move.

There will no doubt be purists who are shocked that one of the central planks in the official Rugby Union ethos has just been ripped out by the nails, but such a change had to come. The original laws were no longer adequate for the IRB to rule with the consent of the governed. In the 1920s, laws prohibiting anything other than strict amateurism for rugby were valid and easy to enforce because they were akin to prohibiting a desert tribe from going to a swimming pool. Apart from a couple of mid-sized League puddles, there weren't any.

Seventy years on, the tribe goes on but the environment has changed. There are now swimming pools opening everywhere—all beckoning the tribe in for a quick dip. For the tribal elders to do anything other than permit the odd swim would be to invite either open revolt or decimation by desertion. Swimming pools aren't such a bad thing, after all . . . These changes will not mean that those Test players currently on the after-dinner speaking circuit at rugby clubs all over Australia will suddenly start to charge a fee. A weekend in Inverell has its own rewards.

It will not mean that rugby players will suddenly start to do Lowes Menswear ads. The Rugby League boys have already got that kind of commercial territory well colonised and the comparatively limited media coverage of Union does not provide the heavy guns necessary to dislodge them, even if we wanted to.

But it might mean that a guy like young Australian centre Jason Little can, through a coalition of now permissible activities, start to receive at least some reward for the $80 000 or so that his loyalty to Union has cost him this year.

It might mean that Phil Kearns, the equally young Test hooker who has just started a job with a sports promotion company, will now be able to do some deals involving himself instead of being unfairly barred by anachronistic regulations. The upshot of it is that for 99.9 per cent of the rugby ranks it will be 'no business' as usual, while for the rest the official rules now allow them to treat, with the same moral code that is good enough for the rest of the population, all those proposals coming at them.

PLAYERS, UNITE: NOTHING TO LOSE BUT YOUR COACHES

Brothers of the Union, we gotta talk. With another football season upon us, the same old struggle with our leaders, our masters, our superiors, now commences. I refer, of course, to our coaches. As you know, they're an exceedingly difficult breed. Just as political leaders who rise to power without votes from the people become horrible dictators, so too the coaches. Mini-Mussolinis all.

Invested with powers above and beyond those of mortal men, the coaches have reigned unchallenged over us footballers since Pontius Pilate first played guest fullback for Jerusalem. Moreover, in the past two millennia our net political gains against these tyrants has been, upon due calculation, precisely zero. The result is that we of the broken noses and cauliflower ears remain an inferior, subjugated class.

Throughout the week, we are made to perform all sorts of humiliating, difficult and unpleasant tasks at the coaches' behest. On the weekend, we are herded on to the field to do battle against each other. Weekly, we thrash each other to a standstill, then retreat to lick our wounds in order to do it all over again next week.

If perchance we are injured in the process, do we get any sympathy? Is the bear in the woods the Pope? The coaches simply call in their medical experts, and we are hung down, brung down, strung down, poked, prodded and pulled until our tortured bodies reluctantly respond, and then we get to go on to the field to belt again, and get belted, next weekend. Brothers, I ask you, how long are we going to put up with this state of affairs? I propose a Footballers' Charter, along the lines of this:

OF YOU, THE COACHES, WE, THE FOOTBALLERS, DEMAND:

1 A little bit of human kindness, dammit. We are not

174

beasts to be yelled at, at your whim. We are not to be publicly humiliated simply because we can't touch our toes or do more than twenty successive push-ups. After all, we don't do them during the games either, so get off our backs.

2   A commitment to use real English to us instead of that guttural, mangled, football-speak. 'Ged-upyermongrel-dog and hit-hit-hit the bags howbaddoyawannit?' may be intelligible to us through long experience, but it is not nearly as civilised as 'Come on now, get up, you can do it, yes you can, hit the bag, you've got to be motivated'.

3   A commitment to stop trying to make us hate each other. How much longer do we have to listen to the likes of, 'We're going to go out and belt these Gordon bastards!' Really. This sort of stuff is straight from the dark ages. For you, the coaches, now is the time to pull your head out from the bowels of your ancient preju-dices and breathe the fresh air. Look around you. It's 1993 and the sun is shining. We don't need that sort of stuff any more.

4   An admission that there are other things to do on weeknights than be at football training. And a solemn promise that the absolute top-limit a football training session will go on for is 90 minutes. It is an immutable fact of football training that you the coaches can have quality or you can have quantity. You cannot have both. Most footballers would infinitely prefer the hard yakka of a brief gut-busting session to the thin strudel of a long-winded session that stretches unendingly into the night. Get it right. Ninety minutes, and to all a good night.

5   Finally, we demand from you an acknowledgement that, yes, meteorological conditions are factors to be considered when choosing what sort of training should be pursued. Coaches whose eyes gleam when the oval turns to mud and know they can devise exercises that will involve their charges rolling around in it should be forthwith taken out and shot. 'No pain, no gain' is rightly the principal plank of any fitness program.

That's just and equitable. But nowhere is it written, 'No discomfort, no gain.' That stinks.

WE'RE AS MAD AS HELL AND WE'RE NOT GOING TO TAKE IT ANYMORE.

Brothers, that's about it for the charter. Now, all sign and give it to your coach. If he still resists, then nail it to his forehead.

WHY IS THERE NO WOMEN'S RUGBY TEAM?

Sent off! On yer bike. Hit the *road* . . . And no further correspondence will be entered into. That's what it might have felt like for Australia's women rugby players when they found out that Australia is to miss out on going to the inaugural Women's Rugby Union World Cup to be held in Wales next month.

But for one small problem. There are no women rugby players in Australia. And therein lies something of a mystery. For while no fewer than 200 players will be fielded from twelve nations, including the United States, Japan, New Zealand, France, Sweden and the Soviet Union, in the World Cup, our own fair land will not be represented at all.

Why is this so, Julius? How is it that, while every other male bastion in sight has been stormed by women long ago, in Australia there hasn't been even a gentle tapping on rugby's door trying to get in? Oh sure, for many women (and no small amount of men) rugby is no doubt viewed as a muddy Neanderthal pursuit unworthy of their attention, let alone their active participation. But similar attitudes will not stop the women of Japan, for example, from fielding what is considered a first-rate women's rugby team in the World Cup. Normally, one might have thought that those famous traits of our national character—sporting, laconic, unpretentious, physical and egalitarian (all in all, a really thuper, thuper bunch of people)—would translate well into a virile brand of women's rugby here.

But so far, not a sausage. Or almost not. The only two rope ladders thrown over the rugby Rubicon as yet have been a female referee, Julia Wells, who until recently refereed lower grade games in Sydney—and a woman in a rugby club in Adelaide who, three years ago, played a game in fourth grade on the wing and has never been heard from since.

In the meantime, women's rugby is flourishing elsewhere, most particularly in the United States. There, it is one of the most popular sports on college campuses, especially on the east coast. While the male jocks on these campuses are more often than not taken up with the deadly serious pursuit of American football—which requires total commitment, huge amounts of money and a lot of time—the women have been flocking to rugby's more informal and looser structure.

With knowledge of the rules an optional extra, a rugby team can be put together from scratch in a matter of days and a bare minimum of equipment is needed to get it moving. For those who might wonder what possible attraction there is in women playing rugby (and it's unbelievably sexist of you to do so, but let it pass), Sue Dorrington, 33, who was formerly the leading light of American women's rugby and now anchors the middle of the front row for England, explains. 'We enjoy ourselves,' Dorrington says, quite simply. 'Women play rugby for all the same reasons men play rugby. It's a chance to participate, compete and then socialise afterwards.'

'No longer will women's rugby be a secret,' she says. 'This is history in the making.' (The way she tells it, it makes the signing of the Magna Carta look a pretty paltry affair by comparison.) 'Hopefully, we can even educate a few men. Nine times out of ten they would be converted if they just came to see a game.' But back here in Australia, still nothing. It is not for want of trying on the part of the rugby authorities. For once, in a story concerning a male bastion, there aren't even any good conspiracy theories around about how it's all because of some dastardly male plot to keep the women out.

In fact, women participating in the game would help soften the image of a code that is often viewed as dangerous, and the ARU would be more than happy to see women's teams spring up if only some females, somewhere, would show some interest.

YOU TOO CAN BE PROUD TO BE BLUE

Back in the days of yore—yonks ago, I think it was—
German Chancellor Otto von Bismarck made the famous
remark that 'Italy is no more than a geographical
expression'. He might have been speaking about New
South Wales. For is our state any more than that? Hands
up all those out there who are proud, I mean really proud,
to be a New South Welshman. As I thought, precious few.

Now hands up those who are proud to be Australian.
As I thought, just about everybody. Thus . . . thus, uh . . .
you BHP and Ampol people can put your hands down now
. . . thus, isn't it self evident that here in New South Wales,
our identification goes overwhelmingly towards being Australians, while being from New South Wales counts for no
more than a couple of small carrots? Every season, New
South Wales plays Queensland at Union as it does at
League and every season it is the same. The advantage for
the Queenslanders in both these encounters is that they will
be playing for QUEENSLAND!, while the boys in blue will
be playing only for new south wales.

Such things make a difference, especially when you're
five points down with five minutes to go and you have to,
as we footballers say, dig deep. In the dressing-room before
the game, the New South Wales Union and League captains
simply cannot say *'And I'll tell you what guys!!! We're going
to win this one for New South Wales, we're going to die for New
South Wales, because we love our state, we adore our state, we
worship our state . . . and we are first, last and always, New
South Welshmen!!!'*

It just won't happen. Never has, never will. But it is a
fairly good bet something like it will be going on in the
Queensland dressing-rooms. They're just like that. Is there
a way around this for the New South Wales teams? Not so
as you'd reckon, given the outrageous domination of
Queensland Union and League teams over the past decade or so. (In the past ten years, in the Union, the

Queenslanders have won fourteen games against only six for New South Wales, while in League the margin is Queensland 18, New South Wales 11.)

But there is the obvious solution, which, in Union at least, is being implemented. That is fostering pride in the team itself. Of the League system, I know nought. But in Union, things have changed and Sunday's game comes at a propitious time. Leaving aside the changes in coaches, personnel, tactics, etc., the New South Wales team should be stronger on Sunday than previously because the jersey means more.

Not because the players have some new-found pride in New South Wales—was Gulliver proud to be bigger than the Lilliputians?—but because this year, things are different for the Union team.

For the first time in seven years the team has gone on a long tour. Not only did that allow some cohesion to be developed among team members as they played and trained daily over three weeks, but, more importantly, that tour allowed the team to get through three weeks of solid, unrelenting, unremitting 'palling around'—so important for all successful football teams—and should give the team the strong spiritual base so necessary for success.

Secondly, throughout the six games New South Wales have played so far, they are unbeaten. Tomorrow, they will not only be trying to win the game for its own sake, but also defending what is the bare beginnings of a proud record. Also, and this may sound schmaltzy but what the hell, there is a feeling of some pride in the new name of the team—the Waratahs.

A reincarnation of the name of the New South Wales team in the 1920s, it gives the team no little sense of history, which is yet another thing to draw on in those crucial last five minutes. So that's the Union side of things pretty much wrapped up—the League boys will have to take care of themselves. If the Waratahs don't win tomorrow they will, at the very least, make the Queenslanders hurt more than usual to stop them.

There is still no way around the Waratahs' natural lack of parochialism, but a feeling for the team itself can help to close the gap.

180

KIWIS THROW THE BOOK AT OLD NICK

Back in 1991, in another life, I was in the Wallaby side on a mini-tour to New Zealand just before the brutes dumped me for the World Cup, and the following scene took place in the lead-up to the Test match.

Auckland: It was a serious tactical error. Having agreed to go on a New Zealand talk-back radio program to talk about a recent publication of mine, I decided at the last minute to invite Nick Farr-Jones along for the ride. Farr-Jones is captain of some rugby team called the Wallabies who are over here to play against the Awl Blicks, or some damn thing. And I thought maybe they'd like to chat to him, too.

As a matter of fact they *were* rather partial to the idea. 'Andtonight-wehavewriter-peterfitzsimonsand we have NICK FARR-JONES, THE AUSTRALIAN RUGBY UNION CAPTAIN!'

As they say in the radio game, the switchboard lit up like a Christmas tree, and that was pretty much the last heard of me or my wretched book. And the extraordinary thing was what the callers were saying to Nick.

Typical was one by the name of Louie from Lower Woop Woop, North Island. He said: 'And I just want to say, Nick, that I hope you Wallabies give the All Blacks a really good thumping on the weekend.'

Uh, come again?

'I think that's the only way New Zealand can win the World Cup is if we lose on the weekend and then we can rebuild the whole team.'

And another, Jerry from Upper Woop Woop, said: 'I, like all New Zealanders, used to support totally the All Blacks but that was when they were representative of all New Zealanders and not just Auckland.' (For this

181

Saturday's Test, the All Blacks will have a record eleven players from Auckland.)

Caller after caller, wanting to make sure Nick knew that—proud New Zealanders though they were—their best wishes were with the Wallabies. Nick happened to mention to one of the callers that he had been receiving a lot of mail lately from New Zealanders expressing similar anti-All Blacks sentiments.

This became the leading electronic sports news story for the following day. How times have changed. This time last year—just before the first Test in New Zealand—the Wallaby tour bus was on the way to training when it had to stop for a traffic light. A shout from an upper-storey window attracted the notice of some players, and the frantic waving of the petite grey-haired old lady soon ensured she had the attention of the entire bus. Suddenly, the waving stopped, the smile was replaced by a malicious gleam, and the Wallabies were left to ponder the extraordinary image of this little old lady giving us a one-fingered salute . . . an internationally recognised signal.

It bought home to a lot of us that we weren't up against just one team so much as an entire nation. But no more. The talk-back calls to Nick were not the only manifestations of Kiwi discontent with the All Blacks—they had been going on all week. Last Tuesday, just before the Australia B game, another grey-haired lady earnestly pleaded with three or four of the players to beat the All Blacks on Saturday.

It was the only way she could see, she tearfully explained, that her beloved Buck Shelford could force his way back into the team. 'Just promise me you'll beat them,' she begged. They promised, perplexed as they were.

Just what the All Blacks have done to deserve such treatment from their countrymen is not altogether clear, but there is no doubting the phenomenon is widespread. Just what effect such criticisms have had on the All Blacks remains to be seen, but it just may be that they will play like men possessed. Possessed of the knowledge that if they fail, there is in all probability a national firing squad awaiting them in their dressing-room—with all black blindfolds.

10 OUR LEAGUE COUSINS

SORRY GUYS, BUT IT'S TIME FOR A LITTLE CHAT

Once again, you guys have blown it. Once again, your united political will—this time against the draft system—has been thwarted by the dictates of League HQ at Phillip Street. But not bad enough that you are once again being made to eat double helpings of humble pie, this time you will have to pay for it too, by way of legal fees.

Think back to that meeting you had on a Sunday morning at Souths Rugby League Club early last year, when the draft was first being proposed. As it happened, I was there. Even using my cauliflower ears and broken nose as credentials, you wouldn't let me in because I was a journalist. You wretches.

But no matter. By going round through the kitchen, I was able to hear a fair measure of what was said. Am I mistaken, or were there a hell of a lot of angry players going on and on about how much they hated the draft? You'd never accept it, you said. Something had to be done, you said. Boy oh boy, they weren't gonna get away with it this time, you said. Etc., etc., etc. Now here we are a year later, the draft has been imposed, and after legal proceedings you're left with a $400 000 bill to boot. The clear expression of your united political will at that time has once again not made the slightest impression on how the situation evolved. I mean, *what is it* with you guys?

Every time an issue comes up directly affecting your livelihood, you get together (after a fashion), beat the drum one way or another and then Phillip Street proceeds to do exactly what they were intending to do in the first place. You were against salary caps. They came in anyway.

Do you know of any other group of professionals or workers who have an upper limit on what they can earn? Sure, it's a collective limit and not an individual one, but the overall effect is the same. Plenty of workers have a lower limit and that works to their betterment, but you are the only people politically muddled enough to have such a system imposed on you. You were against the drug tests. You now have them too.

Remember all your fierce pronouncements about how you would never accept such a thing? What happened to them all? To get to the point, let's look at the difference between the political power of you guys and the political power of lumps of coal and see if we can actually spot any difference.

With no disrespect at all—and I mean that, so don't take the comparison badly—I can see little. You players are the raw material in a multi-million dollar industry. *Millions* of dollars change hands as a result of the highly skilled and dynamic entertainment you are providing.

Without you, the League industry would immediately grind to a halt. Without the lumps of coal, the coal industry would grind to a halt as well. But the lumps of coal do not have the capability to withdraw themselves as a raw material. They cannot say where they will go, what price will be paid for them, what treatment they will be subjected to. You guys can, but you don't.

Why is that so? So the court brought down a decision that Phillip Street was legally entitled to impose the draft system. That's no doubt right. But so what? That is not the point.

The point is that you collectively, as a more or less united body, don't want the draft, as the 170 signatories to your suit bear witness. In just about any other group of sporting professionals in the world—most particularly your colleagues in the NFL—that united political will would be enough to stop the project cold. But not here.

The League commands. You follow. It's a mystery to me how you can be so politically naive as to let it continue.

KEEPING UP WITH JONESIE

Dear Balmain Boys: So, you're thinking of taking on Alan Jones, the former Wallaby coach, as a replacement for Warren Ryan next year.

An interesting choice . . . should you go ahead, there's some good news and some bad news.

I write to you as one who first encountered Jones when, as coach of the Manly first grade Rugby Union team in 1983 and coming out of a clear blue sky from places unknown, he took Manly to their first premiership in 32 years.

The following year I also had a brief tenure under his command in the Wallaby team.

Here are a few points about what to expect from him if he does become the coach of your venerable club.

- First, throw away your wrist watches. From his first moments of coaching, your time will be his time. In fact, the rest of your life will become little more than an infrastructure on which to hang your football career—for the greater glory of Balmain, and, only incidentally, of course, Alan Jones.

  Phone calls at all hours of the day and night will be par for the course, to talk about any number of matters, all pertaining to the cause of Balmain ultimately winning the premiership.

- Jones's own energies directed towards winning will be boundless. Though there is no way you will be able to match him in the high energy stakes, make it as close as you can or you will be in reserve grade. Do NOT talk to him about the fact that you promised your girlfriend you'd pick her up at midnight. Do you want Balmain to win or not? Where is your commitment, damn it?

- Your talent alone will not be enough to ensure your spot in the team. In a choice between flair and dogged obedience to the game plan, Jones will pick dogged obedience every time.

- Be prepared for many, many Churchillian speeches exhorting you to bloody and brilliant battle against whoever the foe of the week is. Don't listen too hard to these speeches, or try to analyse them—the magic might not work. Instead, just be swept along in the rhetoric and for a while you really *will* feel as if you can knock over brick walls. (Oh, do ask him to tell you about the time he single-handedly managed to save Malcolm Fraser's prime ministership by giving Big Mal a stern talking to which, to hear Jonesie tell it, gave Fraser the courage to go in and stare down a rebellious Cabinet. A really ripper yarn usually thrown in some-time when the theme will be 'moral courage'.)

- Soon after he arrives at your club you will witness the emergence from within the team of a Jones Inner Circle. There will be no trouble identifying who is in the circle and who is outside—members of the JIC will sort of glow when he's around, and he will glow right back. Membership of the JIC requires total adherence to the JL (the Jones Line) on all matters, and independent thought is not encouraged. If you desire to promote your membership to the JIC then make sure that when Jones cracks a joke you scream with laughter as though your sides would split. If he frowns, look as if your cat has been run over.

  If you are not in the JIC initially, do not despair—the attrition rate within the JIC is very high as either Jonesie gets bored with you or you can no longer hack him.

- Overall, though, never doubt the man's tremendous ability as a coach, in pure terms of achieving results. If you go with him and ignore all else, the League world may very well be at your feet at the end of the season, even if you're ultimately viewed as nesting pigeons atop an enormous statue of Jones.

Good luck
Kind regards

Peter Fitz

IF YOU'RE DOWN ON YOUR RUCK . . .

On tour with the New South Wales team in New Zealand in 1992, I was amazed to see in Wellington's The Dominion *newspaper a diatribe from the former New Zealand Prime Minister, David Lange, about what a boring, class-ridden game rugby was. I penned this reply which the paper published the following day.*

Sorry to be churlish about this, but one cannot allow to pass without comment David Lange's thesis of last Monday that Rugby Union is a crashing bore.

It almost put us players of the New South Wales Rugby Union team—currently on tour in your fair and muddy land—off our Weetbix.

And, simple oaf footballers that we are, it seems only fair that we make an attempt to put Mr Lange off his Weeties in return. So, Mike Moore, Jim Bolger, Sir Robert Muldoon . . .

Do I hear a cry of 'mercy'?

Mr Lange's first point is that no serious television news program should ever begin with a rugby Test loss, as TVNZ did recently.

With due respect to Mr Lange, the fact is that 99.99 per cent of the population are not professional politicians and thus unfortunately retain the tendency of the 'great unwashed' to be interested in all sorts of things that do not even remotely touch on commercial interest rates, new legislation on bottle-caps, and visiting heads of state. Things like the fortunes of the country's most revered football team really interest them. Dreadful, isn't it, how people are?

As one who has suffered no little damage at the hands of the All Blacks, I might add that if given a choice, my news would always be headed by the newsreader saying 'more bad news from the All Black camp today . . .'

Next, Mr Lange says that while Rugby League is good and fast-moving on television, showing off many skills, Rugby Union is none of the above.

Fast-moving, sir? Perhaps, but surely only in the manner of a windmill.

The fact is, League is amazingly repetitive: player takes the ball up, gets belted, falls over, player takes the ball up, gets belted, falls over. Add water, repeat a thousand times till your nose bleeds and voilà, your average league game.

As to the apparent difference in skill levels of the two codes. Mr Lange offers up for denigration the Rugby Union scrum. Sir, even Rugby League's most ardent supporters admit that the League scrum is generally a cross between the Fall of Saigon and a brothel at midnight. Of all parts of the two codes you could have chosen to make a comparison, this was not the one. But moving right along . . .

The All Blacks are 'now named, boorishly after a beer', sniffs Mr Lange. True enough. Uh, but is it not also true that the League people over here are falling over themselves to become part of something called the Winfield Cup? Enough said?

But, on to the strangest claim of all in Mr Lange's article. 'In terms of international competition,' he writes, 'rugby doesn't rate.'

The world's second biggest football code, played in 126 countries, doesn't *rate*? Surely he means Rugby League? Played only in scattered parts of Australia, New Zealand, Papua New Guinea, France and England, Rugby League is little more than a parish pump game with pretensions to an international grandeur it will never possess.

But forget all that for the moment.

Even as we speak, another Lange slander of Union is coming down hard. According to the former PM, 'Union is a poor role-model for young people because of its hypocrisy'.

The terrible 'hypocrisy' Mr Lange names is that 'while League is up front about offering young working men the chance to profit from their ability and commitment' some of the 'Union players are driving around in late-model cars, with no visible means of support'.

Well, whip me hard with wet spaghetti! To think of the truly devastating effect the hypocrisy of all this must have had on young people, as they contemplate life's cruel injustices; it is just too much.

Can Mr Lange be serious that this is the reason rugby is not a good role model for young people?

Anyway, on he goes. The gist of the rest of it is that rugby is a game for 'snobs', a pillar of the establishment, 'administered by fuddy-duddies in London' and 'a bastion of conservatism' to boot. Scary stuff, indeed.

And to think that such a fierce form of political repression has managed to masquerade as a simple, muddy football game for all these years.

Best of all, though, in the same vein, is this: 'If Union ever does go fully professional', he writes, 'it would cast aside the mystique of the elite with which it is enshrined.'

Again, I cannot pass.

What mystique? What elite? I'm here to tell you, sir, the bottom of an All Black ruck is one of the most classless places on this earth. Lenin and Marx would have loved it.

See, never before, when Fitzpatrick and Co. have near rucked me to death, have they first paused to determine my social background, how much I earn, or who I vote for. They just set to with a will and rucked the hell out of me all the same.

And, I dare say, if from some part of New Zealand were to suddenly arise a man, with legs like tree-trunks and feet like rocks, who proved to be even more adept than the others at rucking me to a wet and sticky pulp, then—whatever this man's social standing, religion, race or background—one of the All Blacks would eventually be obliged to stand aside for him so that he, too, could take his turn at me. The brute.

Does anyone doubt that this true classlessness of rugby is so? Can anyone name another fifteen in the country, working tightly together, who can boast such a wide social, racial and religious mix as the All Blacks?

Though an outsider, I should be much surprised, but perhaps Mr Lange can set me straight. I'd be interested to hear.

Apart from all that, I thought his was a good and well-informed article.

As a result of the article I was flown back to New Zealand a couple of weeks later to have a nationally televised debate with Lange.

There were two problems.

- Two days before the debate, I received a very bad gash over my right eye, resulting in stitching and bruising everywhere and making it difficult to argue what a truly great and sophisticated game rugby really was.
- In the make-up room before going on, Lange proved to be an extremely likable and interesting bloke, his article notwithstanding. It made it difficult to get any real venom up for the debate, but we somehow bumbled our way through.